About the author

Kirsten Campbell-Howes has worked in the area of ELT for 16 years. She taught English in the UK and in Shanghai, China. Since then she has been writing and co-writing ELT books and digital products and has been working in this area for over ten years. Her writing includes a popular series for young learners, a series for young teens studying abroad and a General English series for adults.

Collins
English for Life

A2 Pre-intermediate

Writing

Kirsten Campbell-Howes

Collins

HarperCollins Publishers
77-85 Fulham Palace Road
Hammersmith
London W6 8JB

First edition 2013

Reprint 10 9 8 7 6 5 4 3 2 1 0

© HarperCollins Publishers 2013

ISBN 978-0-00-749776-8

Collins® is a registered trademark
of HarperCollins Publishers Limited.

www.collinselt.com

A catalogue record for this book is available
from the British Library.

Typeset in India by Aptara

Printed in Italy by LEGO SpA, Lavis (Trento)

Acknowledgements

The publisher and author wish to thank the
following rights holders for the use of copyright
material:

–Twitter, Inc. for the use of the Twitter logo and text
–Facebook for material from www.facebook.com

Twitter®, Tweet® and Facebook® are registered
trademarks.

If any copyright holders have been omitted, please
contact the Publisher who will make the necessary
arrangements at the first opportunity.

CONTENTS

INTRODUCTION

Collins English for Life: Writing will help you to develop your writing skills in everyday life.

You can use *Writing*:
- as a self-study course
- as supplementary material on a general English course.

Writing consists of 20 units, divided into the following four sections:
- Section 1 Writing to share information
- Section 2 Writing to get things done
- Section 3 Writing for work and study
- Section 4 Writing for pleasure

Unit structure

To make things easy for you, each unit has a similar structure. We recommend that you do the exercises in order when working through a unit. Each unit includes a selection from:
- A 'Getting started' section, which introduces the topic of the unit.
- A 'Looking closely' section to introduce the types of writing we will be looking at.
- 'Language focus' exercises that ask you to practise the language, grammar, styles and techniques presented in 'Looking closely'.
- 'Writing clearly' and 'Get writing' exercises that ask you to practise the language and skills you have learned.

Other features
- There are boxed texts highlighted in green that give you extra information on 'Clear usage' that will help you complete the unit.
- There are also 'Useful tips' and 'Useful vocabulary and phrases' boxes to help you complete the writing exercises.

At the back of the book there are these useful documents:
- Useful phrases for writing formal and informal emails, invitations, reviews, etc.
- Information on sentence structure, punctuation and short forms.
- A checklist for proofreading your own writing.
- A glossary which gives you definitions and example sentences for some of the difficult words in the units.
- An answer key which includes sample answers for all the questions in the book.

How to use this book

There are two ways to use this book:
1 Work through from units 1–20.
2 Choose from the Contents page the units that are most useful or interesting to you.

Language level

Writing has been written to help learners at A2 level and above (Elementary to Intermediate).

Other titles

Also available in the *Collins English for Life* series at A2 level: *Reading, Speaking* and *Listening*.

Available in the *Collins English for Life* series at B1 level: *Reading, Speaking, Listening* and *Writing*.

How to improve your writing skills

Many students think writing is the hardest skill to learn, but this doesn't have to be true. Here are some simple things to do to improve your writing:

1   Read as much as you can in English. Read books, newspapers, magazines, blogs, social media – whatever you can find. Reading lots of different writing will introduce you to new vocabulary and grammar.

2   Practise by writing as much as you can in English. Try writing simple things like lists in English, then move to more complex things like blog posts. Don't expect to be a great writer straight away. Try to practise a little every day and you will soon get better.

3   Learn the rules of English grammar, sentence construction and punctuation. English is a large and complex language, but learning the rules will help you with your writing. Doing the exercises in this book is a good start!

What is 'good' writing?

Not everyone agrees what good writing is, but if you follow the list below, this should help you decide if your writing is good or not:

1   It is easy to understand. This is not the same as 'boring' or 'simple'. Good writing can include lots of different vocabulary and some complex sentences but still be easy to read.

2   It is pleasurable (fun) to read. As well as being easy to read, good writing should 'flow'. This is hard to describe, but means you can follow the text easily without getting confused; there are no gaps or strange sentences that make you stop to read twice and you find yourself wanting to read more and more. Think of a time when you have read something very quickly and can't believe you have finished it already – that is writing which flows.

3   It isn't too long or too short. A 50-page list of instructions on how to turn on a TV is too long; a five-word sentence to say why you want to apply to a course is too short. Good writing will find the balance between being too long and too short.

4   It is communicative (it tells you something you didn't know before). All good writing should communicate something. This might be facts, ideas, opinions or something else.

1 SHORT EMAILS

Getting started

1 How many emails do you send and receive each day?
2 Who do you write emails to?
3 What subjects do you read and write about?

Looking closely

1 Read the emails and answer the questions.

1 What does Lewis want?
2 What does Julie want?
3 Does Julie like comedy?
4 Does Julie like Thai food?

Hey Julie

I hope things are good with you.

What are you doing on Thursday night? I've got a spare ticket for a comedy show in Camden – would you like to come? We could go out for dinner after the show. There's a nice Thai restaurant near the market. Let me know if you're interested.

Speak soon 😊

Lewis

Hi Lewis

How are you doing? Thanks for the invitation – I'd love to see some comedy with you. I don't like Thai food, though. Why don't we go for Italian instead?

See you Thursday!

Julie

Language focus

1 Read the phrases from the emails again. Mark the phrases for making a plan 'P', opening an email 'O', or closing an email 'C'.

1 How are you doing? *O*

2 Speak soon ....

3 Would you like to come? ....

4 See you Thursday! ....

5 I'd love to see some comedy with you ....

6 Why don't we go for Italian instead? ....

7 I hope things are good with you ....

Useful vocabulary and phrases: making plans

Use these phrases to make plans and arrangements	Use these phrases to respond to a plan or arrangement
Would you like to go to the cinema?	Yes, that sounds good.
How about watching a film?	Yes, that sounds like fun.
Why don't we play tennis?	I'd love to!
We could visit the museum.	Thanks. I'll see you there.
Let's go out on Thursday.	Sorry, I'm busy then.
	Thanks but I have other plans.
	Maybe another time?

---

2 Unjumble the phrases for making plans.

1 Wednesday go the Let's cinema on to *Let's go to the cinema on Wednesday?*

2 could football? We play

3 going How to Italian about restaurant? an

4 comedy? and some don't go Why we see

5 park? like work you to go the Would to after tomorrow

Writing clearly

1 Write a reply to each question in exercise 2, using the phrases from the box.

2 Imagine you are the person in each sentence. Write a sentence to make or respond to a plan.

1 a Jack wants to go to the cinema on Saturday with Xiao Li and Adil.

Why don't we go to the cinema on Saturday?

b Xiao Li is too busy to go to the cinema on Saturday.

c Adil doesn't want to go to the cinema on Saturday. He wants to go on Sunday.

2 a Orla would like to go to a Chinese restaurant on Monday with Kate.

b Kate wants to go to a Japanese restaurant instead.

Language focus

1 Read the emails. Which email is formal? Which is informal?

Hey Jo,

What's up? Let's go out this weekend – maybe see a film?

Speak soon!

Love,

Marta xx

Dear Mikael,

I hope you are well.

I'm writing to let you know that the date of your next English class is now Monday 5th June, not Tuesday 6th June.

Please let me know if you can still come.

Kind regards,

Betsy

2 Mark these phrases 'F' for formal and 'I' for informal.

1 Hi / Hey I

2 Dear ....

3 What's up? ....

4 I hope you are well. ....

5 Speak soon. / See you soon. ....

6 Love / Hugs / Kisses ....

7 Kind regards ....

8 x (= kiss) ....

9 Cheers. ....

10 I look forward to hearing from you. ....

Useful tips: informal emails

- Use more contractions such as 'What's up? Let's go out'.

- Use informal greetings such as 'hi' or 'hey'.

- Use informal endings such as 'Cheers' or 'Speak soon'.
  (For really informal emails you can end with the first letter of your name and / or a 'kiss', e.g. 'H. x').

- Use shorter sentences and more informal grammar, e.g. missing out words in a sentence: 'Maybe (we could) see a film?'.

Writing clearly

1 Write an opening phrase and closing phrase for an email to …

1 your best friend

2 your dad

3 a friend you have met once or twice

4 your bank

2   This email has six punctuation problems. Find them and rewrite the email.

> Hey Janet,
>
> How are you. If you re free tomorrow would you like to go to the cinema There's a nice new, Italian place by the river. Maybe we could try it Let me know if you want to go.
>
> xx
> Carrie

Useful tips: formal emails

- Write in full sentences, and try not to use contractions.
- Don't use slang or informal phrases.
- Use formal greetings, such as 'Dear'. 'Hi' is OK if you know the person you are writing to.
- Use formal endings such as 'All the best' and 'Kind regards' or 'Best regards'.

Get writing

1   Write an informal email to arrange an evening out with a friend.

- Ask what he / she is doing next Thursday evening.
- Make a suggestion about something fun to do.
- Make a suggestion about somewhere to eat.
- Choose informal phrases to open and close your email.

2   Write a formal email to your new English teacher to arrange a lesson. Include the following:

- Ask if your teacher is available next Saturday.
- Suggest a time and place for the lesson.
- Choose formal phrases to open and close your email.
- Be friendly and polite.

My review

I can tell the difference between formal and informal emails.   ❑

I can open an informal email.   ❑

I can close an informal email.   ❑

I can write a short email to make a plan with a friend.   ❑

2 LONGER EMAILS

Getting started

1   What is your daily routine?
    What activities do you do most days?
2   Does your daily routine sometimes change? How?
3   Who do you write your longest emails to?

Looking closely

1   **Read the email and answer the questions.**

1   Who is sending the email? Who is receiving it?

2   What is the relationship between these two people?

3   What are some differences between Stan's life in Edinburgh and his life in Toronto?

From	stantheman92@funmail.org
To	alekscicek@lswcorp.ca
Subject:	Hello from Edinburgh!

Hi Aleks

This is my second week in Edinburgh – can you believe it? I love it here. I'm so happy I decided to go to university in Scotland.

Life is very different here. I share a flat with two other students from my course. Each day I get up around 7.30 and walk to the university. On the way I buy breakfast at my local café. Everyone here eats sausages – they're nice, but not very healthy! At university I have classes all morning. My classmates come from all over the world – there are lots of Chinese and Nigerian people. We all eat lunch together in the canteen – usually sandwiches. In the afternoon I study or go for a walk around town – there's so much to see. In the evenings I go out with my classmates, except on Fridays and Saturdays, when I wash dishes at an Italian restaurant. I'm even learning some Italian!

I miss living at home, especially mom's cooking and your stupid jokes ☺ Living in my own flat is great, but I don't like cleaning and doing the dishes. Edinburgh is very small compared with Toronto, and it's cold, even in summer!

I miss you, little brother – write soon!

Take it easy ...

Stan

Language focus

1 Read Stan's email again. Complete the table.

	Stan's daily routine in Edinburgh
Morning	*gets up around 7.30*
Afternoon	
Evening	
Fri / Sat evening	

Useful vocabulary and phrases: daily activities

When you describe your daily activities use verbs in their infinitive form:

In the morning I get up, brush my teeth, have breakfast and go to work.

In the afternoon I have lunch, study and go shopping.

In the evening I go out (with my friends), go to the gym and have dinner.

When you describe another person's daily activities, change the form of the verb:

Stan gets up ... He eats ... He goes out ...

---

2 Change these sentences to the first person (I go / I eat / I have, etc.).

1 He eats lunch at 1.00 p.m.
  I eat lunch at 1.00 p.m.
2 She always gets up at 8.00 a.m.
3 She works from 9 to 5.

4 In the afternoon he goes to the gym.
5 In the evening she works at the cinema.
6 In the evening he studies or watches TV.

3 Fill the gaps in each sentence.

1 Stan ..*walks*.... (walk) to university every morning.
2 Stan's friends ...*eats*.... (eat) sausages for breakfast.
3 I ..*goes out*..(go out) with my friends on Friday nights.
4 We always ...*haves*.... (have) lunch in the school canteen.
5 Stan ...*have*...... (have) dinner at the Italian restaurant on Saturday evenings.

4 Complete the table with information about you and a friend or family member.

	Your daily activities	Your friend's daily activities
Mornings	*I get up at ...*	*He / She gets up at ...*
Afternoons		
Evenings		
Weekends		

5 Choose the best description of each paragraph from Stan's email.

1 The first paragraph …	**a** introduces the email.
2 The second paragraph …	**b** compares Toronto and Edinburgh.
3 The third paragraph …	**c** describes Stan's daily routine.

6 Read the text and mark where each new paragraph should start.

Hi Mum. Thanks for sending me the books – they look very interesting!
I'm having a lovely time here in Granada. The weather is beautiful and
Spanish people are very friendly. Learning Spanish is easy, because no one
wants to speak English! Let me tell you about a typical day here. I get
up at 9am and have coffee and pastries for breakfast. Then Inés, my
Spanish teacher, comes to my house and gives me a lesson. I eat lunch
in a cafe near my apartment. Then I have a siesta – that's the time in the
afternoon when Spanish people sleep or relax. Most of the shops close
for a few hours. In the evening I meet my friend Jorge and we talk or go
for a walk. We sometimes go out for tapas. Spanish people eat very late.
Sometimes I don't go home until 1am! You and Dad should come and visit
me here. You can stay with Jorge's parents. I'll even teach you some
Spanish!
Love Lisbeth

Writing clearly

1 Practise writing paragraphs.

1 Write a short paragraph (1–2 sentences) to start an email to a friend in a different country.

2 Write a paragraph (20–30 words) about your typical morning activities.

3 Write a paragraph (40–50 words) about a colleague. Describe his or her daily activities.

4 Write a short paragraph (1–2 sentences) to close an email to your friend.

Useful tips: punctuation

Your emails will be easier to read if you use:

- a full stop [.] at the end of every sentence.
- a comma [,] to break up clauses in a long sentence.
- a question mark [?] at the end of a question.
- an exclamation mark [!] for excitement about something (but not too often).
- an apostrophe ['] for a contraction (e.g. I'm) or possession (e.g. Stan's job).
- a dash [–] to connect two ideas or give more information.

Language focus

1 Add punctuation to these sentences.

1 I miss you

2 Every day I go to the gym

3 Can you believe Ive been in Rio for two months now

4 Often Peter my friend goes fishing

5 I love Paris its amazing

Get writing

1 Write an email to someone in your family. Describe your daily activities.

- Start with a short introduction. Say something nice about where you live.
- In the next paragraph, describe your daily activities.
- Say what you do at different times of day, what you eat and who you see.
- Close your email. Say something nice to your family member.

Useful vocabulary and phrases: writing home

Hi / Hey	How are you? I hope you're well.
Let me tell you about ...	Let me describe my daily routine ...
Every day I ..., Sometimes I ..., I always ...	In the morning / afternoon / evening, I ...
Life is very different here.	I'm having a great time.
I miss you. / Wish you were here!	Love / Hugs / Kisses

My review

I can use paragraphs to break up text.	❑
I can choose the right verbs to talk about daily activities.	☑
I can use punctuation correctly.	☑
I can write an email with 2-3 paragraphs to describe my daily life.	❑

3 POSTCARDS

Getting started

1 Where was the last place you went on holiday?

2 What did you do there? Did you have a good time?

3 Have you ever sent a postcard? Who to?

Looking closely

1 Read the postcard below and answer the questions.

1 Who is the postcard from?

2 Who is the postcard to?

3 Which activities has Rosie done?

4 What will Rosie do tomorrow?

2 Label the postcard with the words in the box.

address	stamp	P.S.	greeting	signature	message

1 address

2 stamp

3 Signature

4 ....

5 ....

6 ....

Hi Everyone! **1**

I'm having a lovely time here. The weather is amazing — it's so hot!

2 On Tuesday I went to see the pyramids. They were so huge! I took lots of photos for you, Jo. I had a ride on a camel too — that was scary! Yesterday I also walked around Cairo and ate some delicious food at a street market.

Tomorrow I'm going to take a cruise down the Nile on a small boat. I'm so excited — it's going to be fantastic!

Wish you were all here!

Lots of love, Rosie xxx **3**

6 P.S. Remember to feed my goldfish!

4

Jo, Phillip, Kristine & Lee   **5**

213 Sowersby Park, Walthamstow

London, E17 5WD

UK

Language focus

1 Read the sentences from postcards. Mark each phrase 'P' for talking about the past, 'F' for talking about the future, or 'T' for typical postcard phrases.

1 Wish you were here!   T

2 On Tuesday I went to see the pyramids.   P

3 I'm having a lovely time!   T

4 Tomorrow I'm going to go on a cruise.   F

5 We're going to visit the Prado Museum.   F

6 We saw the most beautiful sunset!   P

7 The weather is great!   T

8 Miss you!   T

9 We ate at a great restaurant last night.   P

10 We went diving and saw an octopus.   P

2 Complete the postcard text with phrases from the box.

> Wish you were here!   went to see   ate   weather is   going to   See you   great time

---

Hi Misty

I'm having a ___great time___ in Rome — the ___weather is___ amazing!

Yesterday I ___went to see___ the Trevi fountain. It was really beautiful. In the evening I found a lovely little restaurant and ___ate___ too much pizza!

Tomorrow I'm ___going to___ visit the Vatican.

___Wish you were her___ ___See you___ soon!

love, Trev

P.S. I bought you a lovely present!

Language note

A postscript is a short message you can write at the very end of a postcard or letter. Write 'P.S.' (the short form of 'postscript') and then your message.

Clear usage: simple past tense

We use postcards to tell our friends and family about the things we have done on holiday. We usually use the **simple past tense**. To form the simple past tense, use subject + main verb in the past tense.

*We **visited** the pyramids.*

We saw the most beautiful sunset!

3 Read the postcard. Underline the verbs in the simple past tense.

Dear Guy, Jackie and Mia

We are having a wonderful time in Hong Kong.

Yesterday we took the Star Ferry to Tsim Sha Tsui and went shopping. I bought a jade necklace and Papa bought a silk shirt. Last night we ate in a tiny restaurant — the food was delicious!

Tomorrow we're going to visit Happy Valley to watch the horse racing. Then we're going to eat dim sum.

We miss you!

Lots of love

Mama and Papa xx

Guy, Jackie & Mia

14 Portland Place, Islington

London, N1 2XJ

UK

4 Match the sentence halves.

1 Yesterday we ate   **a** some lions and tigers in the zoo.

2 We saw   **b** British Museum.

3 Lisa bought a beautiful   **c** some delicious seafood.

4 I visited the   **d** scarf in the market.

5 We took   **e** the ferry to Hong Kong Island.

5 Fill the gaps in these sentences.

1 We   ate   (eat) noodles at a Japanese restaurant.

2 Patrick .... (climb) the mountain and .... (see) a snake.

3 We .... (visit) the British Museum and .... (see) the exhibition.

4 I .... (take) a bus to .... (visit) the Tower of London.

5 Yesterday I .... (go) to the market and .... (buy) a silk scarf.

Clear usage: 'going to' for future

When you want to write about plans in the future, use 'going to'.

*I'm **going to** visit the Louvre tomorrow.*   *We're **going to** fly to Laos on Monday.*

You can change 'going to go' to 'going'.

*I'm **going** to the market tomorrow.*   *She's **going** to Kowloon to buy a scarf.*

6   Correct the mistakes in these sentences.

1 We're go to eat at a French restaurant.

2 I'm go to go to the cinema this evening.

3 I think I going to like Cairo.

4 We're going to visited the museum tomorrow.

Get writing

1   Read your holiday plan. Today is Day 3 of your holiday. Follow the instructions and write sentences for a postcard home.

> *Holiday to London:*
> *Day 1: Bus to Buckingham Palace*
> *Day 2: (yesterday) French restaurant*
> *Day 3: (today) shopping*
> *Day 4: (tomorrow) British Museum*

1 Write a sentence about Day 1.   **3** Write a sentence about Day 3.

2 Write a sentence about Day 2.   **4** Write a sentence about Day 4.

2   Use the sentences you wrote in exercise 1 to write a postcard to a friend.

- Start with a greeting and a sentence about where you are and what the weather is like.
- Write about three things you have already done. Use the simple past tense.
- Write a sentence about something you are going to do.
- Write a sentence to close your postcard.
- Write the address.
- Write a postscript (P.S.)

My review

I can identify the main parts of a postcard.	❑
I can write about activities in the simple past tense.	❑
I can write about plans using 'going to'.	❑
I can write a postcard describing a holiday or trip.	❑

4 TEXT MESSAGES

Getting started

1 How many text messages do you send and receive each day?
2 Who do you send text messages to?
3 What do you text about?

Looking closely

1 Read the text messages and answer the questions.

1 Where is Joanne?

2 What is the problem?

3 What does Dee suggest to solve the problem?

2 Match these parts of the text messages to their meaning.

1	r u	a	seven o'clock
2	7	b	I'm sad / disappointed
3	ur	c	laughing out loud
4	:(	d	your
5	u	e	see you
6	c u	f	you
7	LOL	g	are you

Joanne: At the restaurant. Where r u?

me: Huh? I'm at home. Thought we were meeting at 7?

Joanne: 7! No. I'm sure we said 6.

me: Check ur calendar!

Joanne: Oh no! I got the time wrong. Sorry! ☹ Can u come now?

me: I'll be there in 15 mins. Why don't u order now? I'll have the chicken!

Joanne: LOL! Thanks Dee! C u soon!

Language note

A text / text message (or SMS) is a short message sent from one mobile phone to another. Use these phrases to talk about texting:

Send me a text / SMS.

Text me later. / I'll text you later.

I sent you a text / an SMS. Did you get it?

Language focus

1 Read the text messages on page 20 again. Underline the phrase that Dee uses to make a suggestion.

Useful vocabulary and phrases: changing your plans

Use these phrases to make a suggestion

Why don't we go to another restaurant?   Shall we try another restaurant?

How about meeting on Wednesday?   Perhaps we could stay at home?

Let's go to the park.   Maybe we should go out?

If you are changing from one plan to another, you can use the word 'instead'

Why don't we watch TV instead?   Let's go to an Indian restaurant instead.

---

2 Unjumble the sentences for making suggestions.

1 instead? Why we cinema to go don't the

2 another watch film? we Shall

3 to go Japanese a instead. restaurant Let's

4 about Wednesday? How tennis playing on

3 Write a sentence to make a suggestion for each situation.

1 You and a friend want to eat at a restaurant. You suggest Indian food, but he does not like Indian food.

2 Your friend wants to watch some comedy, but you prefer watching films.

3 Your friend takes you to the swimming pool, but it is closed today.

4 You and your flatmate made a plan to go the the park, but it is raining now.

5 Your friend wants to see a film at the local cinema. When you get there, all the tickets for that film are gone.

Useful tips: text speak and emoticons

To save time when you are texting, use text speak to shorten words:

C u soon = See you soon. *Where r u?* = Where are you? *15 mins* = 15 minutes *2nite* = tonight *Gr8* = great *Thx* = Thanks *NP* = No problem *h8* = hate BTW = by the way

Sometimes we leave out all the vowels (and some consonants) to shorten words:

cd = could

Use emoticons to show how you are feeling:

:) = smiling / happy :(= sad / disappointed ;) = funny / joking

Looking closely

1 Read the texts. Underline the text speak and write down what it means.

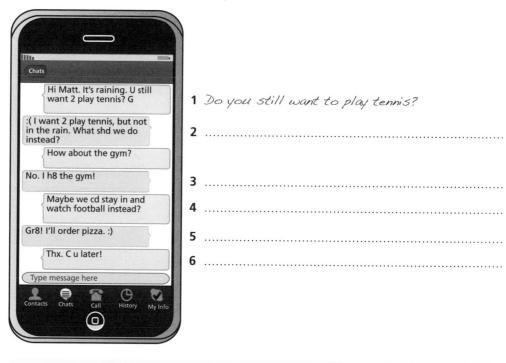

Chats

Hi Matt. It's raining. U still want 2 play tennis? G

:(I want 2 play tennis, but not in the rain. What shd we do instead?

How about the gym?

No. I h8 the gym!

Maybe we cd stay in and watch football instead?

Gr8! I'll order pizza. :)

Thx. C u later!

Type message here

Contacts   Chats   Call   History   My Info

1 *Do you still want to play tennis?*

2 ....

3 ....

4 ....

5 ....

6 ....

Language note

In texts, you can miss out some of the words in a sentence to save time.

At the restaurant. = I am at the restaurant. Sorry. = I am sorry.

You can miss out verbs like 'do' and 'have' from the start of a question.

U still want 2 play tennis? = Do you still want to play tennis?

U got a ticket 4 the concert? = Have you got a ticket for the concert?

2 Practise making these sentences shorter. Use text speak and miss out words.

1 Have you got any food for dinner?

2 I can't come out tonight. I'm too busy.

3 I'm sorry. I thought we were meeting at 9 o'clock.

4 Do you want to go to the gym tonight?

5 That's great! I'll bring something to drink.

Useful vocabulary and phrases: making suggestions

Let's ...	Maybe we could / should ...
How about ...?	Maybe we could ... instead.
Why don't we ...?	If you like, we could ...

Language focus

1 Circle the correct answer (note: sometimes both answers are correct).

1 I'll be there at / in ten minutes.

2 Are you at / in the cinema?

3 See you at / in the café at / in 30 minutes.

4 I'm at / in the party.

5 Are we meeting at / in 7.30?

Clear usage: prepositions of time and place

Use 'at' to talk about time and place.

Let's meet at 7. See you at 10.30. Are we meeting at the restaurant?

Use 'in' to talk about places you can go inside.

I'm in the car park / restaurant / swimming pool.

Use 'in + time' to talk about how long you will take to do something.

I'll be ready in 15 minutes. We'll be there in an hour.

Get writing

1 Write text messages to suggest plans for each situation.

1 You want to take a friend to the cinema tonight.

....

2 Your friend wants to go out this weekend. You know she likes Italian food.

....

3 It's a beautiful day. You and your friend both like playing tennis.

....

2 Write text messages to answer each text below. Suggest a change in plans.

1 There are no tickets for the cinema 2nite! :(

....

2 Italian food sounds good, but I'm on a diet :(

....

3 Oh no! It's raining. We can't play tennis now. What shd we do?

....

My review

I can understand simple text messages.	❏
I can use text speak and emoticons.	❏
I can make a suggestion for changing a plan.	❏
I can write text messages to make and change arrangements.	❏

5 SHARING NEWS ONLINE

Getting started

1 Who do you like to chat with online?
2 What messaging service do you use?
3 What's the longest conversation you've ever had online?

Looking closely

1 Read the conversation and answer the questions.

1 What does Elodie want Pete to do?
2 Why can't Pete come out?
3 What does Pete agree to do?

Add	**Topic** **Profile** **Call**	**Send File**

Elodie:	Hey Pete. Got 5 mins?	17:05:37
Pete:	Sure. What's up?	17:05:46
Elodie:	Pia and I are going out after work. Want to join us?	17:05:52
Pete:	Where r u going?	17:05:58
Elodie:	Probably the George for drinks. Maybe we could go to PJ's for food later? You should come – it'll be fun!	17:06:01
Pete:	I'd love to, but I have to finish my work. I've got lots to do!	17:06:15
Elodie:	But it's 5! You should come out and have some fun – you work too hard!	17:06:21
Pete:	Well … I suppose I could come out for dinner. Why don't I meet you at PJ's at 8?	17:06:35
Elodie:	Gr8! :) See u there!	17:06:40
Pete:	Cool, c u later!	17:06:50

2 Read the sentences from the conversation. Mark them 'S' for making a suggestion, 'O' for expressing an obligation (something it is a good idea for you to do), or 'SO' for expressing a strong obligation (something it is very important for you to do).

1 Maybe we could go to PJ's for food later? S
2 You should come … ....
3 … I have to finish my work. ....
4 You should come out and have some fun. ....
5 Why don't I meet you at PJ's at 8? ....

Language note

When you greet people online, use the same language as for texting or writing informal emails:

Hey / Hi / Hello   *How're you? How's it going?*
                                                      How're things?

Don't use formal language like 'Dear ...', but it is polite to check if your friend or colleague is free to talk.

Are you free right now?   *Have you got 5 minutes?*

Clear usage: expressing obligation and necessity

For very strong (100%) obligation, use 'must' and 'have to'.
*You **must** visit your grandma more often. I **have to** work late this evening.*
For weaker obligation (50%), use 'should'.
*You **should** come out more often. I **should** stop eating so much chocolate.*

Language focus

1 Complete the conversation with 'should', 'must' or 'have to'.

Kerry: Hey Phil, my boss says I **1** ....*have to*........ work late today. :(I don't think I can come to the party – sorry!

Phil: But you **2** .... come! It won't be any fun without you!

Kerry: But everyone else in my office **3** .... work late. They'll be angry if I get to leave early.

Phil: I think you **4** .... talk to your boss. Tell her this is important.

Kerry: What do you think I **5** .... say?

Phil: Tell her it's your brother's birthday party and you **6** .... go.

Kerry: You're right. I **7** .... stand up for myself. Wish me luck!

2 Read the explanation, then complete each sentence with 'mustn't' or 'don't have to'.

The negative of 'must' is 'must not / mustn't'. It expresses a strong negative obligation. The negative of 'have to' is 'don't have to'. It means that you don't have to do something, but you can still do it if you want to.

1 You .... be rude to your boss. You could lose your job!

2 I .... work late on Fridays, but sometimes I do anyway.

3 We should go away this weekend. I .... work on Saturday.

4 You .... lose this key – it's the only one I have.

5 Ed is such a nice guy. He .... see his grandma so often, but he visits her every weekend.

3 Read the conversation. Underline the phrases for sharing news.

Miriam: Hi Rasmus. Are you free to talk?
Rasmus: Hey Miriam. I'm free. What's up?
Miriam: You won't believe this, but Keira and Jack are having a baby!
Rasmus: OMG!!!! Wow! That's amazing news :) Who told you?
Miriam: Keira told me last night. She also said that it's going to be a girl!
Rasmus: How exciting! I'll send them a card. Oh, I've got some news too.
Miriam: Really? What is it?
Rasmus: I've got a new job!
Miriam: Wow! That's amazing! Congratulations! Let's go out tonight to celebrate ...

Useful vocabulary and phrases: sharing news

Use these phrases to share news

Sarah said that ...

I heard that ...

Did you know that ...?

Did you hear about ...?

Use these phrases to share unusual or exciting news

You won't believe this, but ...

I've got some (exciting) news.

Use these phrases to react to news

OMG! (= Oh my gosh). Wow! Really?

That's great / amazing / shocking / terrible!

Congratulations! (if news is good)

I'm so sorry to hear that. (if news is bad)

Writing clearly

1 Use the phrases from the Useful vocabulary box to share some news. Follow the instructions below.

1 Tell your friend that you have a new job.

2 Tell your friend that two people he / she knows are getting married.

3 Tell your friend that you didn't get the job you wanted.

4 Tell your friend that you are moving to another country.

5 Tell your friend that someone you both know has lost his / her job.

2 Now write a response to each sentence you wrote in exercise 1.

Example: You won't believe this, but I've got a new job! / Really? That's great!

Useful vocabulary and phrases: closing a conversation

Use these phrases to pause an online chat (e.g. if you need to do something else)

Sorry, I have to take a call. Just a second.

I'll be back in a minute. / BRB (= be right back)

To close (finish) a conversation politely use one of these phrases

Sorry, but I've got to go now. / I'd love to talk more, but I have to go.

It was nice chatting to you.

Let's talk again soon.

Language focus

1 Use the phrases from the Useful vocabulary box to close the conversations. Remember to be polite.

1

Mia: The party was fun, and everyone wanted to know about my new job.

Me: ....

2

Simon: Work's been really busy. I have so much to do before Friday!

Me: ....

3

Sophia: I'm having a great time in Spain. You'd love it. How are you anyway?

Me: ....

Get writing

1 Write responses to these sentences.

1 Hey, what's up. Are you free to talk?

2 They are going to get married!

3 Anne told me that she lost her job!

4 I'll be back in a minute.

5 I'd love to talk more, but I have to go.

My review

I can greet friends online and end a conversation.	❏
I can use 'should', 'must' and 'have to' to express obligation.	❏
I can use different phrases to share and respond to news.	❏
I can chat with friends online.	❏

6 FILLING IN FORMS

Getting started

1 When was the last time you filled in a form?
2 Where do you normally have to fill in forms?
3 What's the most important form you've ever had to fill in?

Looking closely

1 When you move to a new city, you often have to fill in forms to register for new services. Circle the places where you usually have to fill in forms.

doctor's surgery   clothes shop   supermarket

pizza restaurant   gym   bank

school / college   dentist   work

library   hairdresser

2 Read the form and answer the questions.

1 What is the first name of the person filling in the form?
2 Is the person filling in the form a man or a woman?
3 Why is the person filling in the form?

Fairside GP Clinic
New Patient Registration Form

Personal information Title: (Miss)/Ms/Mrs/Mr Gender: M/(F)   Date of Birth: |_|_| |0|4| |_|_|
                                                                                      DD   MM   YY

First Name: |L|E|I|L|A| | | | | | | | | | | | | | | | | | | | | | |

Middle Name: |_|_|_|_|_|_|_|_|_|_|_|_|_|_|_|_|_|_|_|_|_|_|_|_|_|_|

Last Name: |_|_|_|_|_|_|_|_|_|_|_|_|_|_|_|_|_|_|_|_|_|_|_|_|_|_|

Primary language: _English_   Nationality: _____   Marital status: (single)/married

Contact information Home Address:

House/Flat no: |_|_|4|_|_| Street: |4|A|D|E|N| |S|T|R|E|E|T| | | | |

Town/City: |_|_|_|_|_|_|_|_|_|_|_|_|_|_|_| Postcode: |_|_|_|_|_|_|_|_|

Email address: |L| . |W|A|T|S|O|N|@|L|E|E|D|S| . |A|C| . |O|R|G| |

Home tel: _0113 343 786_   Mobile tel: _____

---

3 Complete the missing information in the form using words and numbers from the box below.

14	LEEDS	ANNE	British
WATSON	89	L2 3SD	097865643321

Language note

Most forms will ask you for your personal details first. These include:

- Title (e.g. Miss, Mr, Mrs, Dr)
- First name (e.g. Anna, Xue, Megumi, Cristian)
- Second / Family name / Surname (e.g. Smith, Wang, Villa-Lopez)
- Date of Birth / DOB (the day, month and year of your birthday)
- Gender (i.e. male or female)

Language focus

1 Answer the questions with your personal details.

1 What is your full name and title?

2 What is your surname?

3 What is your full date of birth?

4 What is your year of birth?

5 What is your gender?

Language note

Most forms will also ask you for your contact details. These include:

- Your address (house / flat number, street, town / city, postcode).
- Your email address
- Your telephone number (mobile, home, work), often shortened to 'Tel. No.'.
- Some forms will ask for details of your 'Emergency Contact Person or Next of Kin'. This is someone close to you (like your husband / wife, partner or parent).

2 Answer the questions with your contact information.

1 What is your flat / house number?

2 What is the name of your street?

3 What town / city do you live in?

4 What is your postcode?

5 What is your email address?

6 Who is your emergency contact person?

Looking closely

1 Read the declaration on this form. Answer the questions.

I certify that the information I have given in this form is true and complete.

PRINT NAME	SIGNATURE	DATE
SAMUEL PHILLIPS	S.Phillips	12/09/13

1 What does the signature say?

2 What is the full name of the person signing the form?

3 What is the date?

4 What does 'certify' mean?

Language focus

1 Follow the instructions.

1 Write your surname in block capitals.

2 Circle the answer that applies to you. male / female

3 Cross out the answer that does not apply to you. male / female

4 What is your tel. no.?

Get writing

1 Complete the form with Lucie's personal details and contact details.

I'm Lucie Clarke. I was born on July 5th 1986.
I live in Bristol, at 27 Park Place, BR3 2XF.
I'm not married.
My email is l.clarke@freemail.org

Personal details:

Title: _miss_   Last name: _clarke_

First name: _Lucie_

DOB: _5_ / _7_ / _1986_   Gender: _female_   Marital status: _single_

Contact details:

House number: _27_   Street: _Park place_

Town: _____ Postcode: _BR3 2XF_   Email address: _l.clarke@freemail.org_

2 Now practise filling out your details on two different forms.

- Go online and search for 'library registration form' and 'new patient registration form'. Print out one example of each.
- Fill in your personal and contact details.
- Write your signature and the date.

My review

I can fill in a form with my personal details.	❑
I can understand the legal importance of a form and write my signature correctly.	❑
I can answer extended questions on a form.	❑
I can complete a variety of different forms.	❑

7 'TO DO' LISTS

Getting started

1 Do you write lists? What for?
2 Do you write lists by hand or type them?
3 How do you show you have finished something on your list?

Looking closely

1 Read the lists. Fill the gaps with words from the box.

| answer | send | read | buy | pick up | tidy | meet |

'To do' list Monday 17th June

- Go to supermarket
1 .... :
- eggs
- cereal
- washing powder
- birthday card
- 2 .... birthday card to Mike
- 3 .... jacket from dry cleaner
- ~~Take car to garage~~
- 4 .... house

To do items: Friday March 3

- Read and 5 .... emails ✓
- 6 .... Sarah's report ✓
- Call Alan ✓
- Make coffee for 11 a.m. meeting ✓
- 7 .... Jessie and Phil for lunch
- Write office blog ✓
- Tidy desk

2 **Answer the questions.**

1 What is each list for?

2 What is different about the two lists?

3 What tasks has the writer of the first list completed?

4 What tasks has the writer of the second list <u>not</u> completed?

Clear usage: imperatives

Use imperatives to give orders and instructions, or to write tasks in a list.
Imperatives are verbs in their base form. For example: *give, buy, pick up, meet, read.*

Pick up *dry cleaning.*

Buy *flowers for Suzanne.*

Read *emails.*

Language focus

1 **Circle the correct verb in each sentence.**

1 Meet / See Alessandro for lunch.

2 Buy / Pick up dry cleaning.

3 Give / Tidy the house.

4 Buy / Read emails.

5 Make / Send coffee.

6 Go to / Pick up meeting.

7 Meet / Write report.

8 Call / Give Andy.

9 Give / Do the washing up.

10 Buy / Make eggs.

Clear usage: content and function words

Content words are the most important words in a sentence. They give us the meaning. They include nouns, verbs and adjectives.

Read *these* **emails** *and* **answer** *the* **telephone.**

Function words are less important. When you write a list, you can usually miss out the function words.

Read **these** *emails* **and** *answer* **the** *telephone.*

Read emails. Answer telephone.

---

2 **Read these sentences. Underline the function words.**

1 Visit the supermarket and buy some eggs.

2 Please pick up the dry cleaning.

3 Call Michaela, about the party.

4 Read the report and make notes on it.

5 Buy Max a birthday card and send it.

3 Use one of the following function words in each gap. In some gaps, more than one answer is possible.

on	at	the	some	to

1 Please make .... coffee before .... meeting.

2 Buy cereal at .... supermarket.

3 Pick up .... dry cleaning when you are in town.

4 Go to the meeting .... Thursday.

5 Send the email .... Jane.

6 .... meeting starts .... 11.30 a.m.

7 Take .... notes when you are in .... meeting.

8 Do .... washing up and tidy .... house.

Writing clearly

1 Rewrite the sentences from exercise 2 on Page 33 as tasks on a list.

2 Rewrite these long sentences as tasks on a list.

Tidy house.

1 Tidy the bedrooms, the living room and the bathroom.

2 Please take the car to the garage.

3 Please talk to Bradley on the telephone this afternoon.

4 At the meeting, please make some coffee and take some notes.

5 Please buy some eggs, some cereal and a pizza when you are at the supermarket.

Useful tips: lists

When you write a list:

• Put the most important tasks first or highlight them with an asterisk (*).

• Use list software on your phone so you can read and write lists wherever you are.

• Use different lists for different tasks, e.g. one for everyday tasks, one for work, one for school.

• Use bullet points for main tasks and sub bullet points for smaller tasks (e.g. the first list on page 32).

Looking closely

1 Read the list and answer the questions.

My 'to do' list – Saturday.

* Go to shopping centre
* • Buy new dress for party
• Get shoes fixed
** • Buy gift for Sandra ✓
• Buy card?
• Meet Joe + Alix for lunch 12.30 ✓
• Buy wrapping paper for gift

1 What is the most important task on the list?

2 What is the second most important task on the list?

3 What task does the writer decide isn't important?

4 What task is the writer not sure about?

5 What tasks has the writer completed?

Get writing

1 **Imagine you are writing the list in exercise 1 on Saturday morning. Use the bullets to rewrite it in a more organised style.**

• Put the most important tasks first.

• Use sub-bullets for the tasks that involve shopping.

2 **Write two lists.**

1 Write a list of everyday tasks you need to complete this week.

2 Write a list of tasks you need to complete at work or at school this week.

• Use bullet points and sub bullet points.

• Put the most important tasks first.

• Use imperatives.

My review

I can recognise a 'to do' list. ❑
I can use imperatives to write tasks in a list. ❑
I can write a 'to do' list for everyday tasks. ❑
I can write a 'to do' list for school / work tasks. ❑

8 INVITATIONS AND DIRECTIONS

Getting started

1 When was the last time you organised a party?
2 Who did you invite?
3 How did you invite your guests?

Looking closely

1 **Read both invitations. Answer the questions.**

1 What is special about Marie's birthday party?
2 What instructions do the guests at Marie's party have?
3 Who is organising the party for James?
4 What do James's colleagues need to do by 31st August?

MARIE **21!**
IS GOING
TO BE

PLEASE JOIN US

at a SURPRISE birthday
party for Marie

at 7.30 p.m.
on Monday 21st July

at Susanne & Tobias's flat
33a Garner Road,
High Wycombe, HP11 3BD

Please arrive between 7.00 and
7.30 p.m. There will be food,
drinks and cake.
Marie will arrive with Susanne
at 7.45, and we will all sing
Happy Birthday!

Remember: this is a surprise party!
Please don't tell Marie about it!
RSVP: susannenowak@freemail.de

You are invited to a leaving party for James Hawksby. After 5 years, James is leaving us for a new job in London. Join us at 5 p.m. on Thursday 3rd September for tea and cake in the conference room, where we will wish James good luck in his new job.

Please give your money for James's leaving gift to Christine by 31st August.

Sam Rogers
General Manager

Useful vocabulary and phrases: invitations

You are invited to ....

I'm having a party!

Please join us at ...

We're moving house!

Language focus

1 Unjumble the invitations.

1 celebration. at our join Please us wedding *Please join us at our wedding celebration.*

2 birthday invited to are Louise's party. You

3 an party. having engagement are We

4 leaving I'm party. a having

5 birthday 30th me Please at join my party.

6 I'm on November. dinner having Please party a 29th come.

2 Fill the gaps with words from the box.

birthday	married	invitation	invited	housewarming

1 You are .... to Grace and Alex's flat party.

2 Did you get an .... to his leaving party?

3 Please come to my 25th .... party.

4 Siri and Karl are getting .... You're invited!

5 Please come to our .... party at 28 Chester Street.

Clear usage: invitation verbs

Please **join** us at ...

Please **arrive** at / by ...

Please **come** to ...

Please **bring** ...

3 Match the events to their descriptions.

1 engagement party   **a** when a baby is named

2 christening   **b** an event we hold when someone dies

3 housewarming party   **c** when two people agree to get married.

4 funeral   **d** a celebration for when someone stops working

5 retirement party   **e** when someone moves into a new house

4 Circle the correct word in each sentence.

1 We are having a housewarming / christening for our new baby daughter.

2 The engagement / funeral of Alice Martin will be held on 6th May.

3 You are invited to a retirement / housewarming party for Jo Hall, who is leaving us.

4 Please join us at our engagement / christening party. Love, Matt and Rebecca

5 Join us at 25 Kirke Avenue for our funeral / housewarming party.

Writing clearly

1 Write a sentence inviting people to these events.

1 Your next birthday party.

2 A surprise birthday party for your friend.

3 A leaving party for your colleague.

4 A surprise retirement party for your colleague.

Language focus

1 Read the directions to a housewarming party. Mark the party on the map.

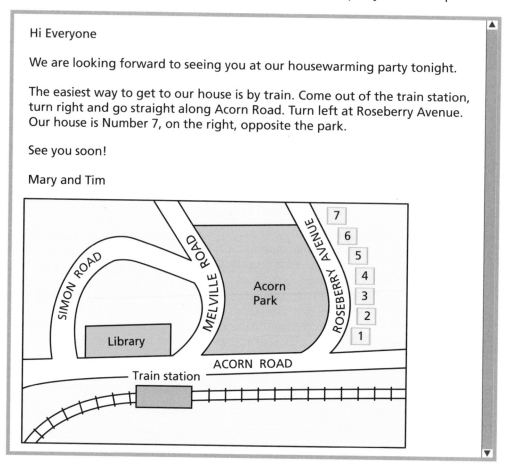

Hi Everyone

We are looking forward to seeing you at our housewarming party tonight.

The easiest way to get to our house is by train. Come out of the train station, turn right and go straight along Acorn Road. Turn left at Roseberry Avenue. Our house is Number 7, on the right, opposite the park.

See you soon!

Mary and Tim

Useful vocabulary and phrases: giving directions

Go straight along / on ...

Cross the road / street.

Turn left at ...

Our house is on the right.

Get writing

1 Look at the map below and complete the directions with language from the Useful vocabulary box.

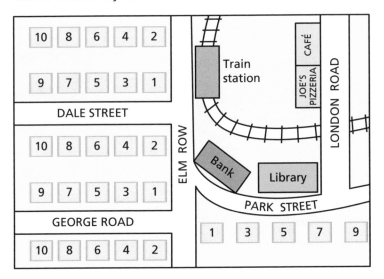

1 <u>Train station to 7 Park Street:</u> Go .... along Elm Row and turn .... onto Park Street. Number 7 is ....·............... the library.

2 <u>Train station to 5 Dale Street:</u> Cross the street and turn left. Turn right onto Dale Street. Number 5 is on the ....

3 <u>Train station to Joe's Pizzeria:</u> Turn left and .... along Elm Row. Turn .... onto .... Street, then turn left again along .... Road. The Pizzeria is on the ...., after the bridge.

2 Write an invitation to your next birthday party.

- Say when and where the party will be.

3 Write an email inviting your friends to a housewarming party.

- Tell them when to arrive.
- Tell them what to bring.
- Give them directions to the party.

My review

I can recognise invitations for different parties.	❏
I can use different phrases to make an invitation.	❏
I can write a set of simple directions.	❏
I can write an invitation to a party.	❏

---

9 ADVERTISING A ROOM

Getting started

1 Have you ever rented out a room in a flat?
2 How did you find new flatmates?
3 Did you use an estate agent, the internet or another service to rent out your room?

Looking closely

1 Read the advertisement for a flat and answer the questions.

1 Who is renting out the room?
2 What sort of flatmate are they looking for?
3 What is the room like?
4 How much money would you need to start renting this flat?

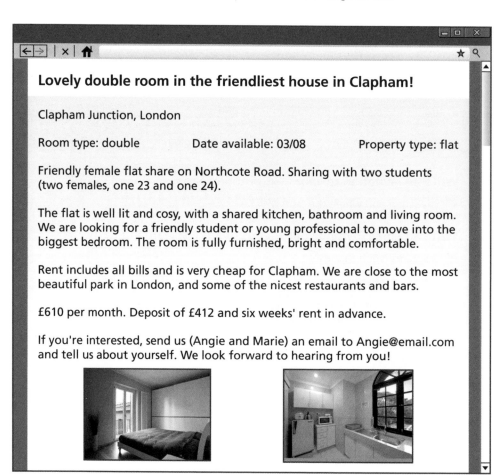

Lovely double room in the friendliest house in Clapham!

Clapham Junction, London

Room type: double   Date available: 03/08   Property type: flat

Friendly female flat share on Northcote Road. Sharing with two students (two females, one 23 and one 24).

The flat is well lit and cosy, with a shared kitchen, bathroom and living room. We are looking for a friendly student or young professional to move into the biggest bedroom. The room is fully furnished, bright and comfortable.

Rent includes all bills and is very cheap for Clapham. We are close to the most beautiful park in London, and some of the nicest restaurants and bars.

£610 per month. Deposit of £412 and six weeks' rent in advance.

If you're interested, send us (Angie and Marie) an email to Angie@email.com and tell us about yourself. We look forward to hearing from you!

2 Label the advertisement with the words and phrases in the box.

location	rent and deposit	headline	availability
contact details	flat / room description		local area information

Useful tips: room advertisements

An advertisement for a room should answer these questions:

- Where is the flat / house?
- What is the room / local area like?
- Who are the other flatmates?
- How much is the rent and deposit?
- How do you get in contact?

Language focus

1 Skim read the advertisement. Which questions in the Useful tips box does it not answer?

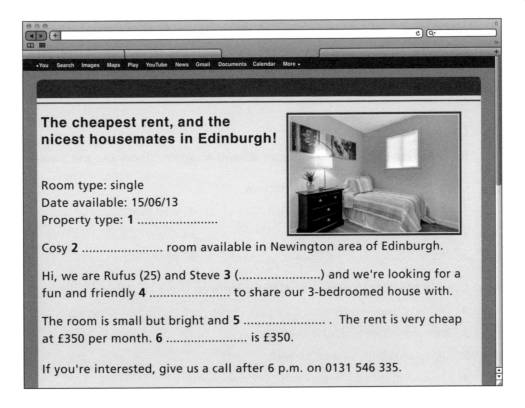

The cheapest rent, and the nicest housemates in Edinburgh!

Room type: single
Date available: 15/06/13
Property type: **1** ....

Cosy **2** .... room available in Newington area of Edinburgh.

Hi, we are Rufus (25) and Steve **3** (......................) and we're looking for a fun and friendly **4** .... to share our 3-bedroomed house with.

The room is small but bright and **5** .... The rent is very cheap at £350 per month. **6** .... is £350.

If you're interested, give us a call after 6 p.m. on 0131 546 335.

2   There is some information missing from the advertisement. Fill the gaps with words from the box.

23	house	fully furnished	deposit	single	housemate

3   Match the terms to their definitions.

1 rent

2 deposit

3 single

4 double

5 bills

6 in advance

a   A room containing a small bed.

b   Before something is needed.

c   A room containing a large bed.

d   An amount of money you give your landlord when you move in. He / She pays it back when you move out.

e   What you have to pay for electricity, water, internet, etc.

f   Money you pay your landlord each month to live in their house / flat.

Clear usage: superlatives

To form the superlative, follow these rules:

For short adjectives, add '-est'
nice > nicest   warm > warmest   light > lightest

For adjectives ending in 'y', miss out the 'y' and add 'iest
cosy > cosiest   lovely > loveliest

For longer adjectives, add 'the most'
beautiful > the most beautiful   comfortable > the most comfortable

Note, some superlatives are irregular (e.g. good > the best).

Language focus

1   Read the advertisements on pages 40 and 41 again. Underline the superlatives.

2   Change the adjectives to superlatives.

1 cosy   *cosiest*

2 comfortable ....

3 nice ....

4 attractive ....

5 cheap ....

6 pretty ....

3   Use the prompts to write complete sentences. Use a superlative each time.

1   Our flat / cheap / in London. *Our flat is the cheapest in London.*

2   The room / comfortable / in the house.

3   The room / good / view of the park.

4   Our local area / nice / restaurants / in Birmingham.

5   The / attractive / parks / in London / near our house.

Useful vocabulary and phrases: renting a room

If you have a room that you want someone to move into

I'm renting out my spare room.

I'm renting out a room in my flat / house.

I'm looking for a new flatmate / housemate.

If you are renting (paying rent each month) for a room in a house / flat

I'm renting a room in a house / flat.

Get writing

1 Turn each adjective below into a superlative. Use each superlative to write a sentence to describe your house, flat or local area.

1 beautiful   *My local area has the most beautiful park in Bristol.*

2 cheap

3 interesting

4 pretty

5 light

6 warm

7 good

2 Read Natalie's description of her flat. Write an advert for her spare room.

My flat is in the Clifton area of Bristol. It's quite expensive: £650 a month, but it's very comfortable. It's a fully furnished double room with a lovely view of the park. I need another girl to share with me: I'm a 22-year-old student – very fun and friendly! There are lots of great restaurants in Clifton – it's a very nice area. The deposit is £800 and all bills are included in the rent. You should email me if you want to know more: natalie@newmail.org

3 Now think about the flat or house you live in now. Write an advert for one of the rooms.

- Say where the flat / house is.
- Describe what the room / local area is like.
- Say who the other housemates / flatmates are.
- Say how much the rent and deposit are.
- Explain how to get in contact.

My review

I can understand and use vocabulary to describe flats and houses. ❑

I can use superlatives. ❑

I can identify missing information in an advert for a flat. ❑

I can write an advert for a room or a flat. ❑

---

10 GIVING AND GETTING ADVICE

Getting started

1 Have you ever moved to a new town or city?

2 Have you ever moved to a new country?

3 What did you do to find out about your new home?

Looking closely

1 **Read the emails and answer the questions.**

1 Do Duane and Lilian live in Shanghai now?

2 Is Duane happy to go to any kind of restaurant?

3 Do you think Duane can speak Mandarin?

Subject: Moving to Shanghai!

Hey Lilian

Guess what? I've got a new job and I'm moving to Shanghai in two weeks! I can't wait – I'm so excited!

I know you lived in Shanghai for a long time. I'd really like your advice. Where do you think I should live? What are some good places to eat (I'm a vegetarian)? Any other advice?

Thanks and all the best,

Duane

Subject: Re: Moving to Shanghai!

Hi Duane

Congratulations on your new job – that's great news! Shanghai is an incredible city. I'm sure you will love it there!

I suggest you live somewhere quite close to your job. Pudong is nice, but Puxi has nicer places to eat. I think you'd like living in Puxi.

There are lots of great vegetarian restaurants all over the city. I recommend that you try Vegetarian House on Wukang Road – it's great!

Let's see, what other advice can I give you …? You have to learn some Mandarin before you go. Not everyone speaks English. Oh, and you should take the ferry across the Huang Pu River at night – then you can see how beautiful the city is.

Good luck! Let me know how you get on!

All the best,

Lilian

---

2 Complete the information from the emails.

1 Where should he live?

....

2 Where should he eat?

....

3 What else should he do?

....

....

Language focus

1 Read the emails again. Circle the phrases that ask for advice.

Useful vocabulary and phrases: asking for advice

I'd really like your advice. Where / What / Which do you think I should …

What restaurants would you recommend?

Where are some good places to visit?

Can you recommend some nice restaurants in the area?

---

2 Unjumble the sentences asking for advice.

1 live? you should do Where think I

2 restaurants I What at? should eat

3 places What to are visit? some good

4 apartment? think you look should I Where for do an

5 museums you What recommend? would

Useful vocabulary and phrases: giving advice

I suggest (that) you …	You should visit …
I think (that) you'd like …	You have to eat at …
I recommend (that) you …	

---

3 Each sentence has one mistake. Rewrite each sentence to make it correct.

1 I think you'd like live in Pudong.

2 I recommend that you eating at the Happy Duck restaurant.

3 You have to trying the food at Chinese Kitchen.

4 You should to learn some Mandarin before you go to China.

Language focus

1 Complete the table with the words in the box.

| metro | taxi | museum | café | theatre | bus | restaurant | ferry | art gallery |

Food	Transport	Culture
		museum

2 Complete the sentences with the most suitable word from the table.

1 The Grand .... shows some great plays.

2 You should try the coffee at the little .... on Songshan Road.

3 You have to take the .... across the Huang Pu River. The view is amazing!

4 You never have to wait very long for a .... in Shanghai, and the driver will take you anywhere you want to go!

5 I recommend that you visit the Shanghai .... You can see some amazing old jewellery and objects there.

6 The .... is probably the quickest way to get around the city. The trains can be very crowded though.

7 Not every .... serves vegetarian food. You should read the menu first!

8 I suggest you visit your local .... It has some beautiful paintings.

9 I think you'd get to work quickest by .... the Number 35 goes from your apartment to your office.

3 Read the email and make a list of things that Jared suggests to Marcello.

Hi Marcello

So, you're visiting Boston? That's great – it's one of my favourite cities!

As you only have three days I recommend that you walk along the Freedom Trail first. That way, you will get to know the city.

If you get tired you should take a bus or a taxi, oh, and you have to take a ferry to the Boston Harbor Islands – the view is amazing!

There are lots of great seafood restaurants. I suggest you try the Crispy Crab on Louisburg Square. There's a great little café in the market on Clinton Street too – you should go there for coffee.

I also think you'd enjoy walking along the Charles River. It's very pretty.

Have a great holiday. Send me a postcard!

Jared

What to eat and drink	How to travel	What to see

Get writing

1 You have just got a new job and are going to move to a new city in two weeks. Write an email to a friend. Ask him / her for advice.

- Greet your friend and tell him / her about your new job and new home.

- Ask for advice on where to live.

- Ask for advice on what to eat and how to travel around.

- Ask if your friend has any other advice.

- Thank your friend and close your email with a friendly phrase.

Useful vocabulary and phrases: in a new city

I'm moving to Sydney ... in 2 weeks.   I think you'll like living in ...

Any other advice?   I recommend you eat at ...

Boston is a great city.   The best way to travel around is to take the ...

---

2 Think of a city that you know well. Your friend is moving there soon and wants some advice. Write him / her an email.

- Congratulate your friend and say why you like the city.

- Give some advice on good places to live.

- Give some advice on good places to eat and to visit.

- List the best way(s) to travel around the city.

- Wish your friend good luck and close your email with a friendly phrase.

My review

I can talk about food, travel and culture in a new place. ❑

I can ask for and give advice. ❑

I can write an email asking someone for advice on a new place. ❑

I can write an email giving someone advice on a new place. ❑

---

11 COURSE APPLICATIONS

Getting started

1 Have you ever applied for a course at a school, college or university?
2 What questions did they ask you?
3 What did you say about yourself?

Looking closely

1 Read the application form and answer the questions.

1 Where has Alison studied Spanish?

2 What kind of school is Alison applying for?

3 What does Alison want to do after this course?

Instituto de España   APPLICATION FORM

Name: A l i s o n H o d g e s   **Age:** 1 8

Qualifications: I t a l i a n : B , F r e n c h : A , H i s t o r y : B

Hobbies and interests: L e a r n i n g E u r o p e a n l a n g u a g e s ,
t r a v e l , r e a d i n g

Tell us a little about yourself and your past experience.

> I am a motivated and hardworking student. I am currently in the
> sixth form at Lee Bridge College. Last year I got an A in my
> French exam. In 2012 I travelled for six weeks in France, Spain
> and Italy and practised speaking all three languages. I have studied
> Spanish to Intermediate level using self-study books and CDs and
> I have also watched many Spanish films.

Why do you want to study at Instituto de España in Manchester?

> I love studying languages and learning about new cultures. I have
> studied some Spanish by myself, but now I want to study Spanish
> properly, at Instituto de España in Manchester. My goal is to study
> French and Spanish at University. One day I hope to live and work
> in South America.

---

2 Write two lists using information from the application form.

Things Alison has done in the past.   Things Alison wants to do in the future.

Got an A in her French exam.

Clear usage: past simple

Form the past simple with subject + past tense verb (verbs can be regular or irregular).
Use the past simple tense to talk about achievements you completed in the past.

I **passed** my exams last year. I **got** 2 'As' and a 'B'.

I **studied** engineering at University.

In 2011, I **went** to Moscow to study Russian.

Language focus

1 Read the application form on page 48 again. Underline sentences in the past simple tense.

2 Now circle sentences in the present perfect tense, then read the Clear usage box below. Why has Alison used the present perfect instead of the past simple?

Clear usage: present perfect

Form the present perfect with subject + have / has + past tense verb. Use the present perfect tense to talk about achievements that you began in the past, and which you are still working on.

I **have studied** Italian for two years.

I **have** always **wanted** to speak Urdu fluently, so I**'ve started** taking advanced classes.

I **have travelled** to many countries (use the present perfect if you plan to keep travelling, or if you travel to other countries very often).

---

3 Fill the gaps in these present perfect sentences.

1 I .... studied French for several years.

2 Julie .... lived in Lebanon since 2009.

3 Mauricio .... always wanted to study Japanese.

4 The students .... read a lot of Italian books.

5 He .... enjoyed studying Polish.

4 Rewrite these sentences in the past simple.

1 I have lived in Norway for three years. I lived in Norway for three years.

2 Sasha has studied Portuguese for several months.

3 Alan has travelled in Asia and Africa.

4 I have enjoyed learning about Chinese history.

5 In Chile, I have studied Spanish and Business.

Writing clearly

1 **Read Miguel's CV. It is April 2013 and he has just finished his degree. Complete the two lists below.**

Miguel Ferrar

Education

2009–2013	Degree in Computer Sciences and Maths, Technical University of Madrid
2008	Cambridge First Certificate in English (FCE) Grade B (First School of English, London, UK)

Experience

April–June 2013	2-month placement at En-path Computer Software Ltd. in Berlin, Germany
Summer 2011	Admin assistant at Aquinas Office Tech, Madrid

Completed achievements   _Achievements Miguel is still working on_

Studied at First School of English,
London, in 2008.

2 Miguel wants to apply for a four-week placement at a computer software company in Madrid in July 2013. Complete the sentences in his application form.

a) Tell us about your previous qualifications and work experience.

_In 2008 I_ **1** .... (study) _at the First School of English in London._
_I_ **2** .... (pass) _my Cambridge FCE examination with a Grade B._

In the summer of 2011 I **3** .... (work) _as an admin assistant at Aquinas Office Tech in Madrid._

b) Tell us what you are doing now.

I have been studying at the Technical University of Madrid. I **4** ....
(complete) _three years of my degree in Computer Sciences and Maths._
I am currently .... (work) _on a two-month placement at a computer software company in Berlin._

Language focus

1 Complete the sentences with information about you.

1 One day I hope to _live in Japan._

2 My goal is to

3 My greatest ambition is to

4 I would like to

5 In three years' time I plan to be

Useful vocabulary and phrases: future plans and goals

My dream is to work as a translator.

In the future I hope to travel to many countries.

One day I hope to work in Berlin.

I would like to be an engineer.

In five years' time I plan to be living in Indonesia.

Get writing

1 There are five mistakes in Frankie's personal statement. Rewrite it with no mistakes.

> **Describe your qualifications and experience.**
>
> I took a course in Japanese at the Nippon School in Frankfurt. I have passed with an A. From 2009-2012 I study German, English and History at my school in Frankfurt. I got an A in all these subjects.
>
> During summer 2011 I working as a waiter in a small restaurant. Since 2012, I have worked as an admin assistant in a language school.
>
> **What are your plans for the future?**
>
> My goal is to study Japanese and to live and working in Japan. In three years' time I plan to be living in Tokyo and studying Japanese. My greatest ambition was to be fluent in Japanese.

2 Answer the question: 'Tell us about your qualifications and work experience'.

- Rather than just list your qualifications, describe them in full sentences.
- If you don't have much work experience, write about your other achievements.
- Write 40–50 words.

3 Answer the question: 'What are your goals for the future?'

- Write about your study and work goals for this year.
- Write about one long-term goal (in 3–5 years).
- Write 30–40 words.

My review

I can use the past simple to write about past achievements.	❏
I can use the present perfect to write about achievements I am still working on.	❏
I can use a variety of phrases to talk about future goals.	❏
I can complete an application form for a course.	❏

12 ASKING FOR HELP

Getting started

1 When you don't understand something in class, who do you talk to?

2 How do you communicate with your classmates outside of class?

3 What questions do you ask?

Looking closely

1 Read the text chat between three classmates. Answer the questions.

1 How do you think Alexis, Samira and Mike know each other?

2 What is Alexis confused about?

3 How does Samira help Alexis?

4 How does Mike help Alexis?

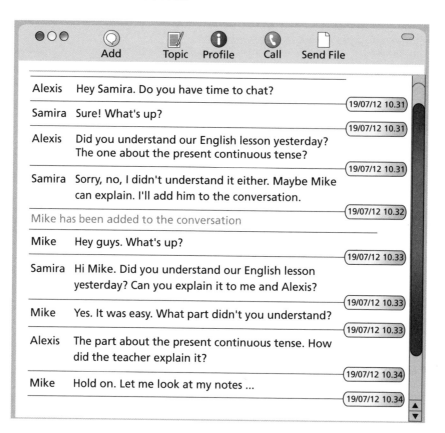

| | Add | Topic | Profile | Call | Send File |

Alexis Hey Samira. Do you have time to chat?
19/07/12 10.31

Samira Sure! What's up?
19/07/12 10.31

Alexis Did you understand our English lesson yesterday? The one about the present continuous tense?
19/07/12 10.31

Samira Sorry, no, I didn't understand it either. Maybe Mike can explain. I'll add him to the conversation.
19/07/12 10.32

Mike has been added to the conversation

Mike Hey guys. What's up?
19/07/12 10.33

Samira Hi Mike. Did you understand our English lesson yesterday? Can you explain it to me and Alexis?
19/07/12 10.33

Mike Yes. It was easy. What part didn't you understand?
19/07/12 10.33

Alexis The part about the present continuous tense. How did the teacher explain it?
19/07/12 10.34

Mike Hold on. Let me look at my notes ...
19/07/12 10.34

2 Read the phrases. Mark them 'A' for asking for help or information, 'RP' for responding positively and 'RN' for responding negatively.

1 What did the teacher say about it? A

2 Did you understand our English lesson?

3 Sorry, I didn't understand it either.

4 I'm not sure.

5 Yes, it was easy.

6 What part didn't you understand?

7 She said that …

8 How did the teacher explain it?

9 What word did she use?

10 I think she meant that …

Clear usage: 'wh' questions in the past simple

'Wh' questions help us get more information when we ask a question. The most common 'wh' questions words are 'what', 'where', 'when', 'who', 'which', 'why' and 'how' (even though 'how' doesn't begin with 'wh' it works in the same way as the other words).

To form a 'wh' question in the past simple, use the question word + did / didn't + subject + main verb.

What did the teacher tell us about modal verbs?

Why didn't he give us any homework?

When did she say the exam was?

Language focus

1 Read the text chat again. Underline the 'wh' questions in the past simple. What other verbs do they contain (apart from the main verb)?

2 Circle the correct 'wh' question word.

1 What / How did she mean when she said 'nouns are naming words'?

2 Why / When did she say the exam was?

3 Who / Which book did Tessa say we should read?

4 How / What did the teacher tell us about adverbs?

5 Which / Why part didn't you understand?

3 Fill the gaps in each question with the correct 'wh' question word. (More than one answer may be correct for some of the questions.)

When	Who	Which	How	Where	What

1 .... word did you use to describe the story?

2 .... exercises did he say we had to do?

3 .... did you answer the questions?

4 .... did he say the next lesson was?

5 .... did you find the answer to the question?

6 .... did you talk to about the homework?

Useful vocabulary and phrases: asking for help

Did you understand ...?

Do you remember ...?

Can you help me with ...?

What did the teacher mean?

Language focus

1 Unjumble the sentences.

1 remember Do what did you yesterday? we

2 homework? help with me you Can my

3 what Do said? teacher remember the you

4 about teacher What adjectives? did the say

5 you understand lesson yesterday? Did our

6 'infinitive' you explain Can means? what

2 Change one word in each sentence to make it correct.

1 Can you understand what she said yesterday?

2 Why did the teacher say about main verbs?

3 Did you explain what 'modal' means? I don't understand.

4 I did understand the lesson. Can you explain it to me?

Useful vocabulary and phrases: responding to requests for help

If you know the answer to your classmate's questions, use these phrases:	If you can't help your classmate, use these phrases:
Let me show you my notes.	Sorry, I can't help.
What didn't you understand / remember?	Sorry, I didn't understand.
	I can't remember.
The teacher meant that ...	I'm not sure.
	I really don't know.

---

3 Write some responses to the questions in exercise 1.

Get writing

1 Use the prompts to write some 'wh' questions in the past simple to your classmate.

1 You didn't understand what your teacher said about modal verbs.

2 You can't remember when you have to hand in your homework.

3 You can't remember where your teacher said your exam is next week.

4 You want to know how your classmate answered the questions in their book.

2 Use the prompts to fill the gaps in this conversation with 'wh' questions in the past simple.

Bella didn't understand her English class yesterday and she wants Felix to help her.

Bella can't remember what her teacher said about how to form the present perfect.

Bella can't remember when she has to hand in her homework.

●○●	Add	Topic	Profile	Call	Send File

Bella Hi Felix.
1 ....
....
11/11/12 13.52

Felix Yes, sure. What part didn't you understand?
11/11/12 13.52

Bella The part about the present perfect tense.
2 ....
....?
11/11/12 13.53

Felix She said you form the present perfect tense with subject + have/has and the past tense form of the verb. Anything else?
11/11/12 13.53

Bella Thanks Felix! You're a star!
3 ....
....?
11/11/12 13.53

Felix On Wednesday next week. Honestly, Bella – you're so forgetful! ☺
11/11/12 13.53

3 Rewrite Felix's responses to Bella in exercise 2. This time, respond using a negative form. Remember to be polite and friendly.

My review

I can use a variety of phrases to ask a classmate for advice or information.	❑
I can respond positively and negatively to requests for advice or information.	❑
I can write 'wh' questions in the past tense.	❑
I can take part in an online text chat about a lesson.	❑

13 JOB APPLICATIONS

Getting started

1 Have you ever had a part-time job? How did you apply for it?
2 Do you have a CV? How often do you update it?
3 Have you ever written a covering letter?

Looking closely

1 Read the advert for a job. Answer the questions.

1 Is the job part-time or full-time?

2 What must you be / have to get this job?

3 What skills are useful for you to have to get this job?

4 What will the company do to help the assistant with the job?

SHOP ASSISTANT REQUIRED

▸ Mode Fashions requires a weekend shop assistant for immediate start.

▸ Duties include serving customers, keeping the shop tidy and taking payments.

▸ You must be friendly and have a neat appearance. Many of our customers are tourists so language skills would be helpful.

▸ Experience preferred but not essential. Training provided.

Email jane@mode-fashions.co.uk with your CV and a short covering letter.

---

2 Match the phrases to their meaning.

1	immediate start	a	The employer will show you how to do your job.
2	experience preferred	b	The employer would prefer it if you have done this kind of work before.
3	not essential	c	You look clean and tidy, with nice clothes and hair.
4	training provided	d	The job begins right away.
5	neat appearance	e	You do not need to have this.

Language note

When you apply for a job, you usually send the employer a CV and a covering letter. You can do this as a letter or (more often) by email.

CV = curriculum vitae (British English), résumé (American English)

Your CV should list your qualifications, work experience and contact information.

Your covering letter should say how you heard about the job and summarise why you should get it.

3 Read the CV and covering letter from Angus, who is applying for the job at Mode Fashions. Complete the checklist for Jane, the Manager at Mode Fashions.

Angus Smith CV
Contact details
Address: 14 Winston Park Road, Brighton B1 7RG
Phone: 0773564677 Email: angus.smith256@speedymail.co.uk
Qualifications
- 2011–2012 NVQ Business and Administration from Brighton Business College
- 2011 A-levels: French (B), English (A), Maths (B)
Work Experience
- 2010–2011 Worked part time as a shop assistant at Comfy Sofas, Brighton. I served customers, ordered new sofas and arranged the window displays.
- 2009 Summer job as a waiter at La Pizzeria, Brighton. I served food and drink to the customers, kept the restaurant clean and took payments.

From   angus.smith256@speedymail.co.uk
To   jane@mode-fashions.co.uk
Subject: Shop Assistant job at Mode Fashions

Dear Jane

I saw the Shop Assistant job advertised in the Brighton News today and I would like to apply for the position.

This September I start my degree in Business and French at the Open University, and I am looking for a part-time job while I study. I have worked in a shop and in a restaurant before. I am very friendly and I enjoy serving customers. I have a neat appearance. I can also speak French and some German.

Unfortunately I am going on holiday for a week from tomorrow, but I can start after that.

I look forward to hearing from you.

Best regards

Angus

Mode Fashions Shop Assistant Checklist

Do they have ...
1. experience? ☑
2. a neat appearance? ☐
3. a friendly personality? ☐

Can they ...
1. start immediately? ☐
2. speak any foreign languages? ☐
3. serve customers? ☐
4. take payments? ☐

4   Angus's CV is very simple. CVs can have several different sections.
Match the CV headings to their descriptions.

1	Contact details	**a**	A list of people who will recommend you.
2	Qualifications	**b**	A list of the jobs you have had.
3	Work experience	**c**	A paragraph that summarises your skills and goals.
4	Hobbies and interests	**d**	Your address, phone number and email address.
5	Personal statement	**e**	A list of things you do that aren't work or study (e.g. sport).
6	References	**f**	A list of the exams you have passed and the grades you got.

Language note

Many CVs start with a personal statement – a paragraph about main skills and goals for the future. It is a summary of the CV. A personal statement should:

- Contain positive adjectives to describe you, e.g. confident, hardworking, reliable.
- Say what your main skills are.
- Say what your goals are, e.g. I am looking for a sales job.

5   Fill the gaps in Angus's personal statement. Use words from the box.

serving	friendly	tidy	degree	experienced	waiter	using	goal

I am an **1** .... shop assistant and **2** .... I am hardworking,
3 .... and reliable. My skills include **4** .... customers, **5** .... a till,
and keeping my working area neat and **6** .... My **7** .... is to get part-time
work in a shop while I study for my **8** .... in Business and French.

Looking closely

1   Read this covering letter. Complete the table comparing Angus and Megan's
applications. Who do you think is suitable for the job – Angus or Megan, or both?

From	megan.jones@freemail.co.uk
To	jane@mode-fashions.co.uk
Subject:	Shop Assistant position

Dear Jane

My friend Alice told me about the Shop Assistant position at Mode Fashions.
I think I would be perfect for this job. I am studying Fashion Design at art college and am looking for a job in fashion.

I have worked at several restaurants so I can serve customers and use a till.
I have also worked in an office doing admin work. Unfortunately I can't speak any foreign languages, but I love fashion and always have a neat appearance. I am friendly and hardworking. I can start work immediately.

Kind regards

Megan

	Angus	Megan
work experience in a shop	Yes	No
other work experience		
languages		
immediate start		
other notes		

Get writing

1 Imagine you are Megan. Write a 40–50 word personal statement for her CV.

   1 Choose three positive adjectives to describe Megan.

   2 Summarise her work experience.

   3 Say what her future goals are.

2 Write your own personal statement. Use the prompts above to help you.

3 Now write your CV.

- Start with your name at the top, then your contact details
- Add your personal statement
- List your main qualifications
- List your work experience

4 Write a covering letter / email to apply for the Shop Assistant job at Mode Fashions.

- Say how you heard about the job.
- Read the advert again. List the skills that match the job advert (e.g. language skills).
- Say if you can start immediately.

Useful vocabulary and phrases: applying for a job

I heard about the job from …

I am a hard-working person.

I have worked as a waitress / teacher / shop assistant.

I enjoy talking to customers.

I can start work immediately.

I look forward to hearing from you.

My review

I can read and understand a job advert. ☐

I can write a personal statement. ☐

I can write a short CV. ☐

I can write a short covering letter. ☐

14 TAKING NOTES

Getting started

1 When you are in a class or at work, do you take notes?

2 Do you write notes in full sentences or do you shorten them?

3 Do you use any special symbols?

Looking closely

1 Read part of a lecture on the left. Compare it to the notes on the right. Answer the questions.

1 What is the lecture about?

2 How does the writer make his / her notes shorter than the lecture?

3 Do the notes cover all the important information in the lecture?

<u>Today we're going to talk about English. Where did this language come from, and how did it develop?</u> The first thing about English is that it comes from many different, older languages. These include Anglo-Saxon, Old Norse, Old French and Latin. The word 'English' comes from the Angles who travelled to Britain in the 5th century. They came from Germany bringing their language 'Anglo-Saxon' with them. Before the Angles came to Britain, most people spoke a Celtic language called 'Brythonic'. The second thing about English is that it has lots of words. The Collins English Dictionary includes around 260,000 words! Many of these words come from other languages. We call these 'loanwords'. An example is 'coffee' which comes from Arabic. Another example is 'pyjamas', which comes from Hindi.	*English: Where it comes from + how it developed* *1. Many diff. older langs. ⟶ English (incl. A-S, Old Norse, French, Latin). Angles came to Britain in 5th C. They brought A-S lang. with them. B4 Angles, Brits spoke Celtic lang. called 'Brythonic'.* *2. English = big vocab. Collins Dic. contains 260K words! Many words from other langs = loanwords, e.g. coffee = Arabic; pyjamas = Hindi*

2 Match the languages to the places they come from.

1 Anglo-Saxon   a Nordic countries such as Norway and Sweden

2 Old Norse   b Countries such as Egypt, Morocco and Lebanon

3 Latin   c Part of Germany

4 Brythonic   d India

5 Arabic   e Italy (old language which was spoken in Europe in Roman times)

6 Hindi   f Celtic countries such as Ireland and Scotland

> **Language note**
>
> Use symbols to write more quickly when you take notes. For example:
>
> C means 'century' $\neq$ means 'is not equal to'
>
> K means 'thousand'   + means 'and' or 'plus'
>
> e.g. means 'for example' $\rightarrow$ means two things are connected
>
> = means 'equals'   / means 'or'

Language focus

1 Read the notes on p. 60 again. Circle the symbols.

2 Rewrite the notes as full sentences.

1 German + French $\rightarrow$ English *German and French are connected to English.*

2 3 + 7 = 10

3 In the past British people spoke Brythonic / Latin. *British people they wer spok Brythonik/*

4 There are Hindi + Arabic words in English. *yes ₭ Latin there is.*

5 Angles + Romans --> British people *= vro*

6 5 + 3 $\neq$ 9

7 'difficult' $\neq$ 'bad' *= hard*

8 'glad' = 'happy' *=*

3 Rewrite these full sentences as notes.

1 The Chinese language is not the same as English.

2 Eight plus ten is not equal to twenty. *8 + 10 ≠ 20*

3 Old Norse is connected to English.

4 At school we can study English and History or English and German.

Language note

'To summarise' means to write down the most important parts of what someone else said or wrote. To write a summary:

- use only the most important information
- keep it short
- it's ok to change some words, except for names and important terms.

Looking closely

1 Compare the full sentence with the two summaries. Answer the questions.

Full sentence	Summary 1	Summary 2
The Angles moved to Eastern parts of Britain in the 5th century. They taught their language, which was called Anglo-Saxon, to the British people.	The Angles brought the Anglo-Saxon language to Britain.	In the 5th century, the Angles came to Britain and the British people began to learn Anglo-Saxon.

1 What information is missing from Summary 1?

2 What information is missing from Summary 2?

3 Which words are different in Summary 1? *brought*

4 Which words are different in Summary 2? *came learn*

2 Write your own summary of the full sentence in exercise 1. Try to make it different from Summary 1 and Summary 2.

3 Write summaries of each paragraph below.

1 In the 11th Century, a group of people called the Normans, who came from Northern France, came to Britain. They brought their language, Old Norman (a kind of old French) to Britain. Many people in Britain learned to speak this language.

2 New words are added to English all the time. For example, five years ago no one talked about 'social media' or 'Tweeting' – now these words are in the dictionary.

Useful tips: taking notes

When you take notes in a meeting or over the phone miss out any unimportant words:

Please call Tony this afternoon at 2 p.m. → *Call Tony at 2 p.m.*

Also shorten any long words:

languages → *langs.*   *British* → *Brits.*

Language focus

1 Imagine you are taking notes in a meeting or over the phone. Shorten the sentences.

1 Can I book a table for two people at 8 o'clock tonight, please? *Table for 2 at 8p.m.*

2 For the meeting can you get two white teas, one black coffee and two white coffees please?

3 After this meeting I'd like Jenny to call Bob and Nick to write a report for Sara, please.

4 I'd like to buy three copies of the Collins Dictionary of English please.

5 Can you email Chris and Phil and ask them to come to a meeting next Tuesday?

Get writing

1 Read these workplace conversations. Rewrite them as notes.

- Miss out unimportant words
- Shorten long words

1 In a meeting (you are taking notes):
Alex: I think we should move to a new office. This one is too expensive.
Shelly: I don't think that's a good idea. Everyone is happy here, and moving offices is expensive too.
Alex: Let's email Mary and ask her what we should do.
Shelly: OK. Let's do that.

2 Over the phone (you are the assistant):
Customer: Hi, I'd like to order a pizza, please.
Assistant: Sure. What kind of pizza?
Customer: A cheese and tomato pizza, please.
Assistant: OK. Where should we deliver it to?
Customer: 25 Armagh Road.

2 Read this classroom lecture. Rewrite it as notes.

- Summarise the long sentences.
- Shorten words if you can.
- Use symbols to help you.

> English is a difficult language to learn. There are several reasons for this. The first is spelling: many English words are hard to spell because English does not have a simple way to write down its sounds. This means it is hard to guess spelling from pronunciation and hard to guess pronunciation from spelling!
>
> English is also difficult because it has lots of homophones. Homophones are words that sound the same, but have a different spelling and meaning. For example, 'they're is spelled T-H-E-Y-apostrophe-R-E and means 'they are'; 'there' is spelled T-H-E-R-E and tells us where something is.

My review

I can read and write simple note-taking symbols.	❏
I can summarise full sentences into notes.	❏
I can use shortened words.	❏
I can write lectures and work conversations as notes.	❏

15 PROBLEMS AT WORK OR SCHOOL

Getting started

1 Have to ever written to your teacher about a problem?
2 Has your doctor ever had to write you a 'sick note' for your school or work?
3 Do you find explaining a problem easy or difficult?

Looking closely

1 **Read the emails and answer the questions.**

1 What problem does the writer of each email have?

2 What solution does each writer suggest?

From   sarbjit.bakshi@freecom.org
To   geoff.wheaton@freecom.org
Subject: Off sick

Hi Geoff

I'm afraid I'm not feeling very well today. I have a cold and I don't want to give it to anyone in the office.

Would it be OK to take a day off work? If I'm still sick tomorrow, I will work from home.

You can call me if you need to ask any questions about work.

Thanks

Sarbjit

From   kassia.gryzbowski@smail.com
To   sally.hughes@englishschoollondon.co.uk
Subject: catching up

Hi Sally

I'm sorry that I missed two classes last week. My mother in Poland was ill, so I had to fly home and see her.

I am back in London now. I would like to catch up on the lessons I missed. Should I do any of the exercises in my textbook?

See you in class on Tuesday.

Best regards

Kassia

---

2 Read the phrases from the emails. Label them 'DP' for describing a problem or 'SS' for suggesting a solution.

1 I'm afraid I'm not feeling very well today. ....

2 I'm sorry that I missed two classes last week. ....

3 I would like to catch up on the lessons I missed. ....

4 If I'm still sick tomorrow, I will work from home. ....

5 Would it be OK to take a day off work? ....

6 I have a cold and I don't want to give it to anyone in the office. ....

7 You can call me if you need to ask any questions about work. ....

8 Should I do any of the exercises in my textbook? ....

Useful vocabulary and phrases: apologising

I'm sorry that ...

I'm afraid that ... (use this to give some bad news)

I apologise for ...

Sorry about ... (this is more informal)

My apologies / Apologies.

I'm so sorry.

Language focus

1 Unjumble the sentences.

1 about doing not homework. Sorry my

2 email. to I forgetting for send apologise the

3 work I'm can't afraid come to today. that I

4 I off take I'm that to have sorry a day work.

5 Friday. class apologise missing on I for

2 Write a sentence apologising for each problem.

1 You forgot to call your boss yesterday.

2 You couldn't go to English classes last week.

3 You forgot to do your homework.

4 You didn't have time to send an important email to your colleague.

5 You are late for work twice in one week.

Clear usage: first conditional – suggesting a solution to a problem

When you have a problem and you need someone's help, use the first conditional to suggest a solution. Use 'If' and the **present simple tense** to describe the problem.

If I'm late for work tomorrow ...

Use 'will' and the base form of the verb to suggest a solution.

If I'm late for work tomorrow, I'll do extra work in the evening.

You also can put the solution before the problem (you don't need a comma).

I'll get up early tomorrow morning if I can't finish my homework tonight.

3 Read the first email on page 64 again.

1 Underline the sentences in the first conditional.

2 Circle the problems in the 'if' parts of the sentences.

    a still being sick tomorrow / taking the day off work

    b needing to ask questions about work / calling his boss

3 What solutions does Sarbjit suggest?

4 Choose the best word to complete each sentence.

if	will	I'll	I

1 .... I take a day off tomorrow, I'll work on Saturday.

2 If I miss another class, ... do some extra homework.

3 If I don't come to the meeting this afternoon, I .... read your meeting notes.

4 I'll take some extra classes .... I fail the test.

5 .... will come to work early tomorrow if I can't finish my work tonight.

5 Complete these first conditional sentences.

1 If I don't come to work tomorrow, ...   **3** I'll do extra work if ...

2 If I don't pass my English test, ...   **4** I will come to work early if ...

Looking closely

1 Read the emails below.

1 Which email is more polite?

2 What phrases does the writer use to make the email polite?

> Hi
> I didn't have time to give you my report yesterday. I was very busy with customers all day.
> I'm also very busy today. I won't have time to write the report today either.
> Andy

Hi Sharon

I'm sorry that I didn't give you my report on time yesterday. I was very busy talking to customers all day and I'm afraid I didn't have time to finish my other work.

I'm also very busy with customers today. If you need the report today, I'll cancel my meetings and finish it as soon as possible.

Please let me know what you'd like me to do.

Kind regards

Andy

2 Rewrite these sentences to make them more polite.

1 I didn't have time to give you my report yesterday.

2 Let me know what you'd like me to do.

3 I didn't have time to finish my other work.

4 I'm too busy to write the report today.

Useful tips: explaining a problem

- It's polite to apologise for a problem, even if it isn't your fault.

- Don't write too many short, direct sentences. They can sound rude.

- Ask the other person if there is anything else you can do.

Get writing

1 Write an email to your teacher to ask for extra time to complete a task.

- Explain what the problem is.

- Say why you are too busy to complete the task on time.

- Use first conditional sentences to suggest a solution to the problem.

2 Write an email to your boss to ask for some time off work.

- Explain why you need some time off.

- Use a first conditional sentence to suggest what you will do to catch up if your boss gives you time off work.

- Be very polite.

My review

I can write a polite apology.	❑
I can use the first conditional to negotiate.	❑
I can write an email asking for extra time to complete a task.	❑
I can write an email to ask for some time off work.	❑

16 PERSONAL PROFILES ON NETWORKING SITES

Getting started

1 Have you ever joined a networking site for work?

2 Have you ever joined a site for making new friends?

3 How do you describe yourself to other people online?

Looking closely

1 Look at the two profiles. Answer the questions.

1 What kind of website is Alex writing for?

2 What kind of website is Sarah writing for?

3 What adjectives do Alex and Sarah use to describe themselves?

| Home | **Profiles** | Jobs | Training |

Alex Minton

Project Manager

Belfast, Northern Ireland

Summary

I'm a confident, hardworking Project Manager with five years' experience working in the construction industry.

I have managed some very large projects for important companies. I have great communication skills and I enjoy working in a team.

I'm looking for new job opportunities. Please send me a message if you'd like to know more.

Click to contact

My self-summary

Hi. I'm Sarah.

I'm a fun-loving music student from Beijing. I love all kinds of music (I play guitar and cello). I'm kind, confident and generous. My favourite things are travelling, animals and – of course – my family.

I'm hoping to meet new people in Singapore. I enjoy going out to music concerts and to the movies. I also like chatting over coffee and going shopping.

If you think we could be friends, send me a message!

Name: Sarah Wang
Age: 21
City: Singapore

Useful vocabulary and phrases: describing yourself

I'm a kind person.

I'm generous / musical / fun-loving.

I love / enjoy / like ...

My favourite things are ...

I'm hoping to meet ...

Language focus

1 Sort these adjectives into groups.

confident	ambitious	musical	hardworking	fun-loving
shy	generous	experienced	qualified	kind

More suitable for work	More suitable for friends	Suitable for both
hardworking		confident

2 Choose the most suitable adjective from exercise 1 to complete each sentence.

1 I'm an .... restaurant manager. I have managed restaurants for eight years.

2 I'm very .... I play the piano, flute and drums.

3 I'm a .... lawyer. I graduated with a first in law last year.

4 I'm a very .... person. I always give 100% to every project I work on.

5 I have no problem talking to new people or starting difficult projects – I'm very ....

6 My friends say I'm a .... person. I love to laugh and have a good time.

7 I am quite a .... person. I try to help other people and I spend a lot of time with my friends and family.

8 I suppose I'm quite .... I find it difficult to meet new people – I don't know what to say!

9 My friends say I'm quite .... I give a lot of money to charity.

10 I want to be Managing Director of my own company. I guess you could say I'm quite ....!

3 Choose the five adjectives from exercise 2 that describe you best. Write one sentence with each adjective to describe yourself.

Clear usage: writing about achievements

Your *strengths* are things that in general, you do well.

I have **excellent communication skills**.

I am **hardworking** and **confident**.

Your *achievements* are things that you have succeeded in in the past.

I have **five years' experience** as a manager. (= I've worked as a manager for 5 years.)

I'm a **qualified** lawyer. (= I passed some exams and became a lawyer.)

---

4 Unjumble the sentences.

1 writing excellent I skills. have

2 ambitious and I'm confident.

3 a three waiter I experience years' have as

4 qualified I'm project manager. a

5 Read the description. Write some sentences for Alana's personal profile on a work networking site.

Useful tips: describing yourself online

- Talk about your strengths, not your weaknesses.
- Be careful not to sound too 'proud' (i.e you think you are better than other people).
- Look at other profiles on the site to see what other people are writing.
- Be honest, but don't share too much information.
- It's important to sound interesting!

Get writing

1 Read these Tweets then use the prompts to write responses.

1 Retweet (RT) this Tweet.

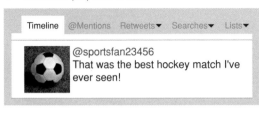

....

....

2 Write an appropriate reply to this Tweet.

....

....

3 Write an appropriate reply to this Tweet.

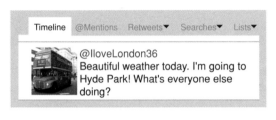

....

....

4 Write another reply to @KathrynAnneW. Tell her about the story in @radioheadfan476's Tweet and share the link with her.

....

....

2 Use the prompts to help you write Tweets. Remember – no more than 140 characters.

1 Use news websites to help you write a Tweet. Find an interesting story, add a headline and link to it, and include a hashtag (#) if there is room.

2 Write a reply to someone on Twitter. Go to Twitter and search for a friend or for a celebrity you like. Read some of the person's Tweets, choose one you like and write a reply.

3 Tweet about a celebrity or a sports event. Search online for a good story then summarise it into an interesting headline and add a hashtag (#).

My review

I can identify different types of Tweet.	❏
I can summarise information in no more than 140 characters.	❏
I can comment on news or current events.	❏
I can write and respond to a variety of Tweets.	❏

19 SOCIAL MEDIA

Getting started

1 Which social media sites do you use to talk to friends?
2 Do you like to share your news online?
3 Do you often comment on other people's posts?

Looking closely

1 Read the Facebook wall and answer the questions.

1 Why is Anja happy?

2 How does Anja know Christopher?

3 How is Darren feeling? Why?

4 What does Georgina mean when she says 'check out'?

2 Label the wall with the words in the box.

comment 'Like' button profile picture post link tag

Language note

Each person on social media networks has a **profile**, with pictures and personal information like their name and location. Under the personal information there is a **timeline** (also called a '**wall**'). The timeline shows everything a person has **posted** on the social media network, with the newest post at the top.

People post lots of different things to their timeline, including photos, videos, text and **links**. You can **tag** your friends in posts. 'Tagging' means putting their name in your post or on a picture.

Language focus

1 Fill the gaps in each sentence with the bold words in the Language note.

1 Did you see the picture I .... on my wall last night? It's so funny!

2 I like to share .... to interesting news stories on my timeline.

3 I don't put much information in my Facebook .... Just my name and hometown.

4 Be careful who you .... in posts and photos on social media network sites. Not everyone wants you to share their information.

5 I think the .... is my favourite part of Facebook. I love being able to see what I was doing months or even years ago.

2 Read the text from some posts on a social media network. Decide if each post is mainly 'C' for a comment, 'S' for sharing information, or 'R' for a request.

1 I can't believe you posted that pic! It's brilliant! ....

2 Interesting story. Thanks for sharing. ....

3 I'm moving house on Friday. Can anyone help me to move some furniture? ....

4 Check out this story about a girl who sailed around the world by herself. ....

5 There's a scary film on at the Rio cinema tonight. I don't want to go by myself. Who'll come and hold my hand? LOL! ....

Useful tips: posting on Facebook

- Try to write in the same tone – if the post is funny, write a funny comment, if it's a link to a serious news story, write a serious comment.

- Keep comments short. If you want to write something long, write a blog post and then link to it on your Facebook timeline.

- Remember that you can comment on your own posts as well as other people's.

3 Read Julie's original post, then number the comments in the correct order, 1–5.

Julie Duncan
Great dinner party last night with Matthew Burrows, Kristina Svenson, Ken Chu and Jamie Wagner. Thanks for helping me cook, everyone!
Like • Comment • Share   3 hours ago in Chicago

6 people like this. 👍

Matthew Burrows I agree with Kristina Svenson. It was such a great evening! Julie, what was the name of the cake you made? It was delicious!
Like   3 hours ago

....

Julie Duncan OK, Matthew and Ken, I've put the recipe on my blog here: http://www.juliesblog.blogland.co.uk/cake-recipe
Like   👍 2   3 hours ago

....

Julie Duncan Aww! Thanks guys! I'm glad you had a good time. Matthew, the cake was a plum and raisin cake. I can give you the recipe if you want!
Like   3 hours ago

....

Kristina Svenson It was a great evening, Julie. Thanks so much!
Like   3 hours ago

......*1*.......

Ken Chu I want the recipe too, Julie. That cake was the best!
Like   3 hours ago

....

4 Choose the best caption for each photo. Write the letter of each caption under the photo.

a Cameron running the half marathon yesterday. So proud of him!

c Everyone having a great time at Miranda's party.

b Mr Tibbles looking very cute and fluffy

d Grandpa's 85th birthday!

....

Language note

A caption is a short piece of text on what you can see in a photo. We often write captions in the present simple or continuous tense, even if the photo shows an event from the past.

John at his graduation ceremony. Shelly winning the 800 metres swimming race.

Get writing

1 Write an appropriate caption for each photo.

1 .... 2 ....

2 Read these posts and write appropriate comments for each of them.

Matthew Burrows

I've got a spare ticket to see Coldplay tomorrow night, because Kristina Svenson isn't well. Who would like it?

Like • Comment • Share   57 minutes ago

Julie Duncan

Our local library is closing down! It's terrible. Where am I going to get my library books from now?

Like • Comment • Share   5 hours ago via mobile

Darren Murphy

Can't believe it's my 25th birthday today! Looking forward to the party tonight!

Like • Comment • Share   5 minutes ago

My review

I can recognise different types of post on Facebook.	❑
I can write appropriate captions for photos.	❑
I can write appropriate comments on other people's posts.	❑
I can make my own posts to the Facebook timeline.	❑

20 ONLINE REVIEWS

Getting started

1 Do you check hotel restaurant and reviews online?
2 If you have a good experience at a restaurant or hotel, would you write a review?
3 Would you complain online if you had a bad experience?

Looking closely

1 Read the reviews then answer the questions.

1 What kind of restaurant is Benny's Diner?
2 What is a 'rating'? Is 4/5 a good rating? Is 0/5 a good rating?
3 What does Gerard mean when he says 'the service is absolutely terrible'?

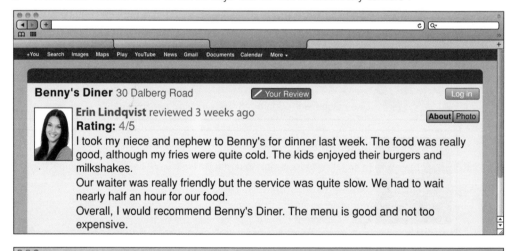

Benny's Diner 30 Dalberg Road   [✎ Your Review]   [Log in]

Erin Lindqvist reviewed 3 weeks ago   [About] [Photo]
Rating: 4/5
I took my niece and nephew to Benny's for dinner last week. The food was really good, although my fries were quite cold. The kids enjoyed their burgers and milkshakes.
Our waiter was really friendly but the service was quite slow. We had to wait nearly half an hour for our food.
Overall, I would recommend Benny's Diner. The menu is good and not too expensive.

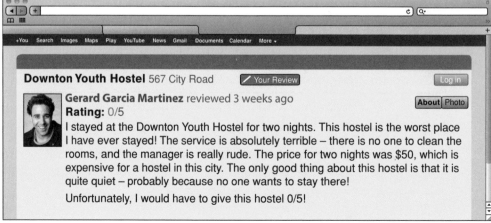

Downton Youth Hostel 567 City Road   [✎ Your Review]   [Log in]

Gerard Garcia Martinez reviewed 3 weeks ago   [About] [Photo]
Rating: 0/5
I stayed at the Downton Youth Hostel for two nights. This hostel is the worst place I have ever stayed! The service is absolutely terrible – there is no one to clean the rooms, and the manager is really rude. The price for two nights was $50, which is expensive for a hostel in this city. The only good thing about this hostel is that it is quite quiet – probably because no one wants to stay there!
Unfortunately, I would have to give this hostel 0/5!

2 Complete the table with good points and bad points from each review.

	Good points	Bad points
Benny's Diner	*food really good, kids enjoyed burgers and milkshakes*	
Downton Youth Hostel		

Clear usage: adverb + adjective

When you review something, you can use **adjectives** to describe it.

*The hotel was **nice**.*

*The food was **bad**.*

*The service was **terrible**.*

You can modify (change) the meaning of the adjective by putting an **adverb** in front of it.

*The hotel was **quite** nice. (It was OK)*

*The food was **really** bad. (really = very)*

*The service was **absolutely** terrible. (absolutely = completely)*

Language focus

1 Read the reviews again. Underline the adverb + adjective combinations.

2 Unjumble these sentences.

1 food restaurant terrible. was The in the absolutely

2 quite restaurant at the food The nice. was

3 Youth The great. was really Hostel

4 very service good. at local is my café The

5 clean. is hotel That quite

6 like I restaurant. Thai really that

3 Use an adverb + adjective combination to write some sentences for reviews.

1 Write a sentence about your favourite local café or restaurant.

2 Write a sentence about a hotel or hostel that you think is 'OK' (but not great).

3 Write a sentence about a restaurant where you had great food or service.

4 Write a sentence about a restaurant where you had bad food or service.

4 Match the nouns to their meaning.

1	service	**a**	the list of food at a restaurant
2	staff	**b**	the people who work at a business
3	youth hostel	**c**	how much you have to pay for something
4	manager	**d**	the person who runs a business
5	menu	**e**	a cheap place to stay, where many people share a room
6	price	**f**	the effort that staff in a hotel or restaurant make for customers
7	waiter	**g**	the score a reviewer gives
8	rating	**h**	the person who serves food at the table

5 Fill the gaps with a word from exercise 1.

1 Hotels in Tokyo are so expensive. I usually stay at a .... instead.

2 The waiter at the restaurant was so rude that I asked to speak to his ....

3 The .... at my local café is quite limited, but the food is very good.

4 The rooms at the hotel were really nice, but the .... was bad, so I only gave it 2/5.

5 This hotel has the best .... from this reviewer.

6 The .... for one night at my favourite hotel is £150.

7 The .... at my favourite restaurant are all so friendly.

8 The .... at my local restaurant is hardworking.

6 Circle the adjective that does **not** match the noun.

1 service: slow, good, clean

2 rooms: expensive, friendly, dirty

3 staff: busy, unfriendly, cheap

4 menu: rude, large, bad

5 prices: cheap, good, large

6 manager: cheap, rude, friendly

7 waiter: busy, slow, expensive

Language note

When we review something and give it a score, we say, for example: 'two out of five' or 'five out of five'. We write this as 2/5 or 5/5.

The meal was just great – I gave it 5/5!

Useful vocabulary and phrases: positive and negative reviews

Use these phrases to write a positive review	Use these phrases to write a negative review
We had a great time at ...	We were very disappointed by ...
We loved / enjoyed ...	
I would (really) recommend ...	I (really) wouldn't recommend ...
The Log Cabin is a great restaurant / hotel.	The Regent is not a very good restaurant / hotel.

7 Change each sentence to make a positive review negative, and a negative review positive.

1 We would really recommend that Brazilian restaurant. The food is great!

2 I was very disappointed by the New Street Hotel. The rooms were really dirty.

3 Tapas Ole! is a good restaurant. The food is nice and the prices are quite cheap.

4 I wouldn't recommend the Charter Street Youth Hostel. The rooms are small and the staff are quite unfriendly.

Useful tips: reviews

- Write about the menu, the staff, the service, the rooms and the prices.
- Use adjectives (was the service good or bad, were the staff rude or friendly?)
- Use some adverb + adjective combinations
- Write positive and negative statements
- Finish with a rating ?/5

Get writing

1 Write a review of a café or restaurant where you have eaten.

2 Write a review of a hotel or a youth hostel where you have stayed.

My review

I can identify good and bad reviews.	❏
I can use adverb + adjective combinations in reviews.	❏
I can express positive and negative feelings in a review.	❏
I can write a short review of a restaurant or youth hostel.	❏

APPENDIX 1 – Useful phrases

1. Emails

Formal emails

Opening phrases	Closing phrases	Notes
Dear Sir / Madam Dear Sir or Madam	Yours faithfully	Use when you don't know the name of the person you are writing to.
Dear Mr / Mrs / Ms / Miss [Family name]	Yours sincerely / Yours truly	Use when you know the name of the person you are writing to but you have never met or you hardly know the person.
Dear [First name]	Best regards / Kind regards	Use when you know the person you are writing to well enough to use their first name.
Hi [First name]	Best regards / Kind regards / All the best	Use when you know the person you are writing to quite well and have a friendly relationship with them.
[First name] / [First name], hi	All the best / Cheers / Best / Thanks	Some people don't like this way of opening an email, but this is quite a popular way to open emails.

Informal emails

Opening phrases	Closing phrases	Notes
Hi [First name]	All the best / Cheers / Best / Thanks	
Hi / Hello / Yo / Hiya / Hey	Cheers / Bye / Speak soon / Later / Hugs / Kisses / [first letter of the person's name]	There are many informal ways to open and close informal emails between friends. These are just a couple.
[no opening phrase]	[no closing phrase]	In informal emails there may sometimes be no opening or closing phrase. This is very common if there are lots of quick emails between two people who know each other well.

2. Making plans and arrangements

Phrases for making plans and suggestions

Would you like to ... ?
How about ... ?
Why don't we ... ?
We could ...
Let's go out on (Thursday) ...
Shall we try another ... ?
Perhaps we could ... go out?
Shall we ... stay at home?

Phrases for responding positively

Yes, that sounds good / like fun.
I'd love to! / I'd love to come.
Thanks. I'll see you there.

Phrases for responding negatively

No, thanks, / Sorry, I'm busy then.
Thanks, but I have other plans.
Maybe another time?

Phrases for changing from one plan to another

Why don't we (watch TV) instead?
Let's (go to an Indian restaurant) instead?

3. Greeting people online

Starting a conversation online

Hey / Hi / Hello
How're you? / How's it going? / How're things? / What's up?

Checking if someone is free to talk

Can you talk?
Are you free right now?
Have you got ... (5 minutes)?

Taking a break from an online conversation

Sorry, I need to take a break.
Sorry, I have to take a call / speak to someone.
I'll be back in a minute.
Hold on a second ... / Just a minute ...
BRB (= be right back).

Ending a conversation online

Sorry, I've got to go now.
I'd love to talk more, but I have to go.
It was nice chatting to you, but I'm afraid I've got to go.
Thanks for the chat. Let's speak / talk again soon.
Bye / Bye for now.

---

4. Sharing news

Phrases for sharing news

Did you know / hear about?
(Sarah) told me that / said that …
I heard that …

Phrases for sharing exciting or surprising news

You won't believe this, but …
I've got some (exciting) news …

Phrases for reacting positively to news

OMG! (Oh my Gosh)
Wow!
Really?
That's great / amazing / brilliant / wonderful!
What great / amazing / brilliant / wonderful news!
Congratulations! / Well done.

Phrases for reacting negatively to news

Oh no! / Oh dear!
Really?
That's terrible / awful / shocking / bad.
What terrible / awful / shocking / bad news.
I'm so sorry to hear that.

---

5. Invitations

Formal phrases for invitations

You are invited to …
We would love it if you could come to …
Please join us at …

Formal phrases for accepting an invitation

We would love to come / join you at …
Thank you. We'd love to come.

Formal phrases for declining an invitation

We would love to come, but (unfortunately) we have other plans.

I'm sorry, but I can't come / join you this time.

Informal phrases for invitations

Join us at … / Come to …

I'm having a party …

We're … moving house / getting married / having a party.

Informal phrases for accepting an invitation

Thanks for the invite. I'd love to come!

Sounds great! We're definitely coming.

See you there!

Informal phrases for declining an invitation

I'd love to, but I have other plans.

Sorry – maybe some other time.

Sounds great, but we can't join you this time.

Sorry I can't make it to your …

---

6. Giving advice

Phrases for giving advice

I suggest that you …

I think that you'd like …

I recommend that you …

You should visit …

You have to eat at / try my favourite …

Phrases for accepting advice

Thanks for the advice.

That sounds like good advice.

Great idea. I'll try that.

That's a good idea.

Phrases for declining advice

I'm not sure about that.

I don't think I'd like that.

Maybe that's not for me.

Thanks, but I don't think so.

7. Talking about future plans and goals

Phrases for describing future plans and goals

My dream / goal / plan / ambition is to ...
In the future / One day I hope to ...
I would like to be a / an ...
In five years' time I plan to be ...

8. Asking for help or information at school

Phrases for asking for help or information

Did you understand ...?
Do you remember ...?
Can you explain / help me with ...?
What did the teacher say / mean?

Phrases for responding positively

Yes, I can help. Let me show you my notes.
Yes, I understood / I remember.
What didn't you understand / remember?
The teacher / He / She / meant / explained that ...

Phrases for responding negatively

Sorry, I can't help.
Sorry, I didn't understand / can't remember either.
I'm not sure.
I really don't know.

9. Apologising

Formal phrases for apologising

I'm sorry that ...
I'm afraid that ...
I apologise for ...

Formal phrases for accepting an apology

Thank you. I accept your apology.
Apology accepted.

Informal phrases for apologising

Sorry about ...
Apologies / My apologies.

Informal phrases for accepting an apology

That's ok.
No problem / No worries.
Not a problem.
Don't worry about it.

---

10. Describing places and people

Phrases for describing places

(Tokyo) is ... fun / interesting / exciting.
There are lots of (interesting people) in ... (Bogota).
(Paris) is probably the most ...
(New York) is (exciting) but ...

Phrases for describing people

People are / Everyone is (friendly) here.
(British) people are ...

---

11. Writing reviews

General

I thought that ...
I went to / tried / ate at ...
In my opinion ...
Let me tell you about ...

Negative

We were very disappointed by ...
I (really) wouldn't recommend ...
I would not recommend (name of place) because ...
(Name of place) is not a very good ...
I was disappointed by ...

Positive

I highly recommend.
We loved / enjoyed / had a great time at ...
I would (really) recommend ...
I would recommend (name of place) because ...
(Name of place) is a great ...
I really liked / loved ...
You really have to try ...
10/10 (ten out of ten = full marks).

APPENDIX 2 – Sentence structure

1. Sentence parts

1.1 Subject, verb, object

The basic English sentence has a subject, a verb and an object.

Kasper loves writing.

In this sentence 'Kasper' is the subject, 'loves' is the verb and 'writing' is the object.

Main clause	This clause has a subject and a verb, and can work on its own as a simple sentence.	*You came!*
Dependent clause	This clause contains a conjunction (linking word), a noun and a verb. It can't work alone as a sentence. It depends on the main clause to tell us what the sentence is about.	*I liked the restaurant **because the food was good.***
Relative clause (also known as a subordinate clause)	This is a type of dependent clause. It begins with a relative pronoun (a linking word like 'which' or 'where') and also has a noun or a verb.	*We saw Alison yesterday, **which was nice.***
Noun Phrase	This is a very basic clause with just a noun or a noun phrase.	***Lunch*** *(noun) was great*

Main clauses and dependent clauses

A dependent clause adds information to a main clause. It starts with a subordinating conjunction (e.g. because) or a relative pronoun (e.g. which). A dependent clause can't work alone as a sentence because it doesn't give us enough information.

Main clause	Dependent clause
Jean wants to go to the Diner	because its her favourite restaurant.

Relative clauses

When a dependent clause starts with a relative pronoun (e.g. that, which, who, etc.), we call it a relative clause.

Main clause	Relative clause
Rachel knows the man	who is sitting at that table.

2. Sentence functions

2.1 Statements

A statement (also called a declaration) tells us some information or what someone thinks. For example:

I saw Jonah yesterday.

That film was great!

Josh said he didn't want to come to the party.

2.2 Questions

A question (also called an interrogative) is always followed by a question mark (?). For example:

What time does French class start?

Who's that man over there?

2.3 Commands

A command (also called an imperative) is an instruction that we give to someone. For example:

Pass me the salad.

I need you to come home right now!

3. Sentence types

3.1 Simple sentences

A simple sentence has a subject and a verb. It is an independent clause. This means that it doesn't need another clause to give more information – it works on its own as a complete sentence.

I like to watch TV in the evening.

3.2 Compound sentences

A compound sentence has two independent clauses. These clauses are linked (connected) by a conjunction (e.g. and, but).

It's Christmas Day, and I'm having a nice time with my family.

I like fruit, but I don't like vegetables.

3.3 Complex sentences

A complex sentence has an independent clause with one or more dependent clauses linked to it.

I liked that film, which is interesting because I don't like comedy films.

3.4 Compound-complex sentences

A compound-complex sentence has one or more independent clauses with one or more dependent clauses.

Tim saw Jules walking down the street, and because she looked so sad, he stopped her and asked what was wrong.

APPENDIX 3 – Conjunctions

Conjunctions are words that link (connect) clauses in a sentence. They are important in writing because they make sentences sound more natural. There are two types of conjunction:

3.1 Coordinating conjunctions

Coordinating conjunctions link two parts of a sentence that are grammatically the same. For example, two nouns or two adjectives. The following table contains the most common conjunctions:

Conjunction	Notes	Examples
and	This is the most common conjunction. Use it to link similar ideas together.	*I like fruit and vegetables.* *She can swim and ride a bicycle.*
but	Use this conjunction to show that two things are different (make a contrast).	*I like fruit but I don't like vegetables.* *She can swim but she can't ride a bicycle.*
or	Use this conjunction to talk about a condition (something that has to happen before something else can happen).	*I don't like fruit or vegetables.* *We can go to the cinema or we can go to a restaurant.*

3.2 Subordinating conjunctions

Subordinating conjunctions link a dependent (subordinate) clause to a main clause. A subordinate conjunction comes at the start of the dependent clause.

Conjunction	Notes	Examples
because	Use this conjunction to give a reason for something.	*I don't like John because he's so rude.* *I can't come to work because I'm ill.*
although	Use this conjunction to contrast two ideas.	*The film was good, although I think the main actress was boring.* *I like Steve, although he does talk a bit too much.*
unless	Use this conjunction to talk about a condition (something that has to happen before something else can happen).	*I won't come to the party unless you come too.* *Unless it stops raining, I'm going to go home.*

APPENDIX 4 – Punctuation

(1) Full stop (US: period) .

Use the full stop at the end of every sentence.

Note: you must start every sentence with a capital letter. *You're a great writer.*

(2) Comma ,

Use it to separate items in a list. You don't need to use it before the last time – use the word 'and' instead.

Please buy bread, milk, butter and cheese.

- Use it instead of the word 'and' in a list of adjectives. *It was a warm, sunny day.*
- Use it to link two independent clauses together with a conjunction. *She was very angry with her son, because he didn't pass his exams.*
- Use it after words like 'however' or 'finally' in a sentence. *Finally, I would like to talk about...*
- Use it to show an interjection (a word or phrase that shows how you feel). *Wow, it's very late! You look beautiful tonight, darling.*
- Use it to separate parts of a sentence that give us 'extra' information. *All my students, and I have many, are wonderful.*
- Use it to separate a dependent clause from an independent clause. *If it keeps raining, we will have to go home.*
- You don't need to use a comma if the dependent clause comes after the independent one. *We will have to go home if it keeps raining.*

(3) Question mark ?

- Use it to show a direct question. *What's your name?*
- You don't need to use a question mark for an indirect question.

She wanted to know when the exam was.

(4) Exclamation mark !

- Use it to show that information is important, exciting or surprising.
  Be careful!
- Try not to use exclamation marks too much.
  They work best in informal writing.

(5) Apostrophe '

- Use it to show a contracted word. *That's my hat.*
- Use it to show possession. *Simon's essay was the best. It was Ladies' Day at Ascot.*
- Use it to show time or quantity. *One week's holiday. In three days' time.*
- Use it to show a shortened date. *He was from the class of '96.*

(6) Single quotation marks ' '

- Use these to highlight a special word or phrase in a sentence.

  Try not to use the word 'and' too much when you are speaking.

- In British English, we use single quotation marks to show that some text or speech is a quote (i.e. was written or said by someone else).

  Shakespeare wrote 'To be or not to be, that is the question?'.

(7) Double quotation marks " "

- In British English we normally use these to show an important word or some quoted text inside some other quoted text.

  The teacher said 'Try not to use the word "and" too much when you are speaking.'

  However, note that in American English (AmE) quote marks are usually used in the opposite way – single quotes appear within double quotes.

(8) Colon :

- Use it to introduce an important or dramatic idea.

  There is only one thing I need: pizza!

  I was so angry: my car had been stolen!

- Use it to introduce a list after a complete sentence.

  There are three things you need to make pizza: dough, tomato sauce and cheese.

- Use it to introduce examples.

  Here are some examples of conjunctions: and, but, or, because.

(9) Semi-colon ;

- Use it to link two independent clauses instead of a comma and conjunction.

  He knew everything about me; I knew nothing about him.

- Use it before adverbs like 'however' and 'finally'.

  The rain stopped; however, we still didn't go out.

- Use it to separate items in a long, complex list where there are already lots of commas.

  The University welcomes some important guests: Professor Ralph, Chancellor, Tutor and Dean of Studies at the University of Stern; Professor Farish, Tutor in English, French and Armenian Studies, Mahler University; and Mr Borge, writer and journalist.

(10) Brackets / parentheses ( )

- Use them to add extra information that is important but not as important as the main information in a sentence.

  Sam was very excited about going to Vietnam (he had never been to Asia before).

- Use them to add your own comments as writer of the text.

  The film (which was very good) was the best part of the evening.

- Use square brackets to explain the grammar or meaning of a direct quote without changing the quote. *'He [David Crystal] is a popular writer on the subject of language.'*

(11) Hyphen -

- Use it with compound phrases that come before a noun and describe it.
  The sixth-form pupils had their exam in the main hall.
- Use it with common phrases.
  My ten-year-old son loves baseball.
  I'd like some step-by-step instructions.
  That milk is out-of-date.
- Use it to write out numbers.
  It's my twenty-fifth birthday.
- Use it to make pronunciation or spelling clear.
  My name is Se-bas-ti-an. S-E-B-A-S-T-I-A-N.
- Use it after a prefix before a name or date.
  He is pro-Obama. The book was written pre-2001.

(12) Dash –

- Use it to make a break in a sentence when you want to make the reader pay attention.
  I won't eat meat – I never will.
- Use it instead of paired commas or brackets.
  He ate the cake – every single piece of it – in less than ten minutes.

(13) Ellipsis …

- Use it to leave a sentence unfinished, often in informal writing
  I'm not sure what to get Tammy for her birthday …
- Use it to show that some words have been left out of a quote.
  'To be or not to be … Whether t'is nobler in mind to suffer …'

(14) Forward slash /

- Use it to show two or more options. Use it instead of the word 'or'.
  We will serve coffee / tea during the meeting.
- Use it in some shortened words.
  w/o = without

APPENDIX 5 – Short forms

Emoticons for texting and instant messaging

:)	smiling / happy
:(	sad / unhappy
;)	joking / don't take this seriously
:D	big grin / happy
<3	heart / love
</3	broken heart / no love
\o/	excitement / jumping for joy
:O	surprise / shocked face
d(^_^)b	headphones / listening to music
(^_-)	winking
o/\o	high five
:-P	sticking your tongue out at someone (cheeky, not rude)
:X	'my lips are sealed' (= I'm not telling you anything)
@}-;--	rose / romantic

Symbols for notes

&	and
+	plus
=	equals / is the same as
≠	does not equal / is not the same as
>	is greater than
<	is less than
"	repeat the text that you see above
@	at
→	connects two ideas
←	connects two ideas
?	don't know / not sure
↑	increasing
↓	decreasing
∴	therefore
#	number
$	dollars / money

Short forms of words

Use these in emails or instant messages to people you know well, as well as to take notes.

abt.	about
b/c	because
c.	circa (around the time)

cf.	compare
ch.	chapter
D.O.B.	date of birth
e.g.	for example
esp.	especially
etc.	and all the rest
govt.	government
i.e.	that is / in other words
max.	maximum
min.	minimum
mth.	month
no. / nos.	number / numbers
N.B.	important
p. / pp.	page / pages
re.	concerning / about
sbd.	somebody
sth.	something
vs.	versus (meaning 'against')
w/	with
w/o	without
yr.	year

Note: You will probably see a number of different ways of writing short forms. A good rule to remember is 'use a full stop if the final letter is missing, but don't if it's present'. So:

st abt yr vs govt

but

c. sbd. max. etc.

Twitter conventions

RT	= Retweet	Use in front of another person's Tweet that you want to share with your followers.
MT	= modified (changed) tweet	Use when you have shortened someone else's Tweet so you can Retweet it. Make sure you don't change the meaning of the original Tweet when you shorten it.
DM	= direct (private) message	Use to send private messages to people that you follow, who also follow you.
@	= at replies	Put in front of the Twitter names of the person you want to send a message to. Note that this message is not private, so anyone can see it.
#	= hashtag	Use it in front of words or subjects so that other people can search for and find Tweets about similar things.
[…]	= square brackets	Use these when you want to add a comment of your own after another Tweet. E.g. RT @ madonnafanclubLondon Great concert last night! [Yes! It was wonderful!]
#FF	= follow Friday	Use this on Fridays to recommend people that you think your followers should follow. For example: #FF @ Ilovecats678 She posts the cutest cat photos on Twitter!

APPENDIX 6 – Proofreading

How to proofread

When you have finished writing a piece of text, you should always proofread it carefully. This means reading your text very closely to check that there are no mistakes and that it reads well.

Step-by-step notes on proofreading

- Print out your text. Use a coloured pen to mark changes on your printed document.
- Read your text, looking for one type of mistake at a time. For example, start by checking your sentence structure. Then start at the beginning again to check your spelling and word choice. If you aren't sure about a word, use your dictionary to check it. Finally, go back and check that your punctuation is correct and that you have used full stops, commas, etc, wherever you need to.
- Next, make sure that the information in your text is correct. For example, make sure you have spelled names of people and places correctly, and that dates and numbers are correct.
- Make sure the formatting of your document is correct. For example, make sure that the font size (e.g. 10, 12) and the font (e.g. Arial, Times New Roman) are the same all the way through. Make sure any headings or notes are in the same style all the way through as well.
- Check the line spacing of your document. This is the amount of space between each line of text.
- Make any changes to your document on screen, checking your marked up printed document.

Tips for proofreading

- Clear your desk of other papers and books so you have a clean space to work on.
- Always proofread from a paper printout, not on screen. It is much easier to see mistakes on a paper printout.
- Proofread in a silent room.
- Never proofread when you are tired or when you have been working on a document for a long time. Look at it the next day instead.
- Don't hurry!
- When you think your document is as good as possible, give it to someone else to proofread. You will be surprised what a 'fresh pair of eyes' can see.
- Don't just use your computer's spell-checker software or grammar-checking software. Humans are much better than machines at seeing mistakes.
- Say the words that you are reading out loud – this will help you to focus on the letters in front of you. It also makes mistakes easier to find.
- Be careful of the ends of lines: watch out for missing full stops, and for words that appear twice by mistake.
- If you make a change in one part of the document, make the same change wherever you find the same mistake. Don't change your mind half way through a document.
- Finally, read your text out loud once more. If you run out of breath, you may need to add more commas and full stops.

MINI-DICTIONARY

Unit 1

busy ADJECTIVE
working hard • *They are busy preparing for a party on Saturday.* unable to do something, because you are doing something else • *Sorry, I'm busy that night, so I can't come to your party.*

comedy NOUN
a type of entertainment that is intended to make people laugh • *His career was in comedy.*

formal ADJECTIVE
very correct and serious rather than relaxed and friendly • *We received a formal letter of apology.*

informal ADJECTIVE
relaxed and friendly, rather than serious or official • *Her style of writing is very informal.*

receive VERB
to get something after someone gives it to you or sends it to you • *They received their awards at a ceremony in San Francisco.*

send VERB
to make a message or a package go to someone • *I sent her an email this morning.*

subject NOUN
the thing that is being discussed in a conversation or a book • *I'd like to hear your views on the subject.*

suggestion NOUN
something that you tell someone they should do • *May I make a suggestion?*

Unit 2

activities PLURAL NOUN
things that you spend time doing • *I have lots of activities planned for the day.*

canteen NOUN
a place in a school where students can buy and eat lunch • *Rebecca ate her lunch in the canteen.*

compare VERB
to consider how things are different and how they are similar • *I use the Internet to compare prices.*

daily ADJECTIVE
happening every day • *...the daily newspaper 'The Times'.*

punctuation NOUN
signs such as ( ), ! or ? that you use to divide writing into sentences and phrases • *You have to give more attention to punctuation and grammar.*

relationship NOUN
the way two people or groups feel and behave towards each other • *The ministers want to maintain the friendly relationship between the two countries.*

routine NOUN
the usual activities that you do every day • *The players changed their daily routine.*

typical ADJECTIVE
used for describing a good example of a type of person or thing • *Tell me about your typical day.*

Unit 3

amazing ADJECTIVE
very surprising, in a way that you like • *It's amazing what we can remember if we try.*

cruise NOUN
a holiday that you spend on a ship or boat • *He and his wife went on a world cruise.*

delicious ADJECTIVE
very good to eat • *There was a delicious menu.*

excited ADJECTIVE
very happy or enthusiastic • *I'm excited to be here.*

fantastic ADJECTIVE
very good • *I read your essay and it's fantastic.*

sunset NOUN
the time in the evening when the sun goes down • *The party began at sunset.*

tiny ADJECTIVE
very small • *My flat in London is tiny.*

Unit 4

consonant NOUN
one of the letters of the alphabet that is not 'a', 'e', 'i', 'o' or 'u' • *The word 'book' contains two consonants and two vowels.*

disappointed ADJECTIVE
sad because something has not happened or because something is not as good as you hoped • *I was disappointed that John was not there.*

instead ADVERB
in the place of someone or something • *Zoe didn't want to go bowling. He went to the cinema instead.*

local ADJECTIVE
in, or relating to, the area where you live • *Susan put an advertisement in the local paper.*

mobile NOUN
a telephone that you can carry wherever you go • *The woman called the police on her mobile.*

perhaps ADVERB
used for showing you are unsure whether something is true, possible or likely • *They lost millions, perhaps billions.*

shorten VERB
to make something shorter • *The treatment shortens the length of the illness.*

vowel NOUN
one of the letters 'a', 'e', 'i', 'o' and 'u' • *The name Emma begins with the vowel 'e'.*

Unit 5

chat VERB
to talk in an informal, friendly way • *I chat to him often.*

conversation NOUN
an occasion when you talk to someone about something • *I had a brief conversation with him.*

express VERB
to show what you think or feel • *Only one company expressed an interest in his plan.*

greet VERB
to say 'Hello' or shake hands with someone • *She greeted him when he came in from school.*

necessity NOUN
a need to do something • *He'd learned the necessity of hiding his feelings.*

negative ADJECTIVE
saying 'no' • *Dr Hunt gave a negative response.* NOUN
in grammar, a form that is used for saying 'no' or 'not', such as 'don't' • *The word 'never' is a negative.*

obligation NOUN
something that you should do • *The judge has an obligation to find out the truth.*

politely ADVERB
in a way that is respectful towards other people • *'Your home is beautiful,' I said politely.*

Unit 6

applicable ADJECTIVE
appropriate or relevant • *Don't fill out this form as it is only applicable to residents of the United States.*

emergency NOUN
a serious situation, such as an accident, when people need help quickly • *Come quickly. This is an emergency!*

fill in VERB
to write information in the spaces on a form • *When you have filled in the form, send it to your employer.*

gender NOUN
the fact of being male or female • *We do not know the children's ages and genders.*

patient NOUN
a person who receives medical treatment from a doctor • *The patient was suffering from heart problems.*

registration NOUN
when something is recorded officially • *I need to fill in a registration form for my local gym.*

surgery NOUN
the room or house where a doctor or dentist works • *My doctor's surgery is only five minutes away.*

title NOUN
a word such as 'Mr' or 'Dr' that is used in front of someone's own name • *After getting married, Julia changed her name from Miss Douglas to Mrs Crawford.*

Unit 7

bullet point NOUN
one of a list of items for discussion or action in a document, marked by round symbol • *Prepare a list of bullet points for the meeting.*

complete VERB
to finish a task • *We will complete the project in May.*

dry cleaning VERB
to clean clothes with a special chemical rather than with water • *We can dry-clean this suit for you today.*

everyday ADJECTIVE
ordinary, a regular part of your life • *Computers are a central part of everyday life.*

imperative NOUN
the base form of a verb, usually without a subject. The imperative is used for telling someone to do something. Examples are 'Go away' and 'Please be careful.' • *I sometimes use imperatives when I need someone to do something urgently.*

instructions PLURAL NOUN
information on how to do something • *The cookbook uses simple instructions and photographs.*

orders PLURAL
the words that someone says when they tell you to do something • *The commander gave his men orders to move out of the camp.*

task NOUN
a piece of work that you have to do • *My task was to cook lunch.*

Unit 8

celebration NOUN
special event organized to mark a birthday or anniversary • *We've planned a big celebration for Martha's birthday!*

colleague NOUN
a person you work with • *She's talking to a colleague.*

invitation NOUN
when someone asks you to go to an event • *I accepted Sarah's invitation to her birthday party.*

invite VERB
to ask someone to come to something, such as a party • *She invited him to her birthday party.* NOUN the act of asking someone to come to something, such as a party • *This letter from John is an invite to his party.*

organise VERB
to plan or arrange something • *We organised a concert.*

party NOUN
a social event at which people enjoy themselves • *We organised a huge party.*

special ADJECTIVE
different from normal, often in a good way • *You're very special to me, darling.*

surprise NOUN
an unexpected event, fact or piece of news • *I have a surprise for you: we are moving to Switzerland!*

Unit 9

area NOUN
a particular part of a town, a country, a region or the world • *There are 11,000 people living in the area.*

advert NOUN
information that tells you about something such as a product, an event or a job • *Have you seen that new advert for that restaurant?*

attractive ADJECTIVE
pleasant to look at • *The flat was small but attractive.*

cosy ADJECTIVE
comfortable and warm • *Hotel guests can relax in the cosy lounge.*

estate agent NOUN
a person whose job is to sell buildings or land • *Our estate agent is having trouble selling our summer house.*

fully ADVERB
completely • *We are fully aware of the problem.*

lovely ADJECTIVE
beautiful, or very enjoyable • *Sam has a lovely voice.*

skim read VERB
to read something quickly and not too carefully in order to pick up the important or significant details • *I'm skim reading my notes from class in preparation for the test tomorrow.*

Unit 10

advice NOUN
what you say to someone when you are telling them what you think they should do • *Take my advice and stay away from him!*

crowded ADJECTIVE
full of people • *He looked around the crowded room.*

culture NOUN
activities such as art, music, literature and theatre • *Films are part of our popular culture.*

ferry NOUN
a boat that regularly takes people or things across water • *They crossed the River Gambia by ferry.*

jewellery NOUN
decorations that you wear on your body, such as a ring on your finger • *She sold all her gold jewellery.*

painting NOUN
a picture that someone has painted • *She hung a large painting on the wall.*

recommend VERB
to suggest that someone would find a particular person or thing good or useful • *I recommend Barbados as a place for a holiday.*

transport NOUN
a system for taking people or things from one place to another in a vehicle • *We will spend the money on improving public transport.*

Unit 11

achievement NOUN
something that you have succeeded in doing • *Being chosen for the team was a great achievement.*

application NOUN
a written request to be considered for a job or a course • *We have not yet received your application.*

apply VERB
to write a letter or write on a form in order to ask for something such as a job • *I am applying for a new job.*

course NOUN
a series of lessons on a particular subject • *I'm taking a course in business administration.*

engineering NOUN
the work of designing and constructing machines or structures such as roads and bridges • *She studies science and engineering at college.*

exam NOUN
a formal test that you take to show your knowledge of a subject • *I don't want to take any more exams.*

fluently ADVERB
easily and correctly • *I speak German fluently.*

goal NOUN
the aim or purpose that you have when you do something • *Our goal is to make patients comfortable.*

Unit 12

communicate VERB
to share information with other people • *They communicate with their friends by mobile phone.*

infinitive NOUN
the basic form of a verb, for example, 'do', 'be', 'take' and 'eat'. The infinitive is often used with 'to' in front of it. • *The infinitive of 'going' is 'go'.*

modal verb NOUN
used, in grammar for a word such as 'can' or 'would' that you use with another verb to express ideas such as possibility, intention or necessity • *A modal verb such as 'might' is useful for talking about the future.*

negatively ADVERB
in a way that means 'no' • *Sixty percent of people answered negatively.*

positively ADVERB
in a way that shows agreement, approval, or encouragement • *We expect both men to respond positively to the challenge.*

studies PLURAL NOUN
the activity of learning about a particular subject • *In 1924, he went to Paris where he continued his studies in painting, sculpture and drawing.*

understand VERB
to know what something means • *'Do you understand what I'm telling you, Sean?'*

Unit 13

appearance NOUN
the way that someone or something looks • *She hates it when people talk about her appearance.*

covering letter NOUN
a letter of introduction sent with a job application • *It's important to write a covering letter.*

immediate ADJECTIVE
happening next or very soon • *There is no immediate solution to the problem.*

part-time ADJECTIVE
less than the full working day or week • *She is trying to get a part-time job in an office.*

preferred ADJECTIVE
liked better or highly appreciated • *I'm looking for a flatmate: non-smoker preferred.*

skill NOUN
a type of activity that needs special training and practice • *You're never too old to learn new skills.*

statement NOUN
something that you write to tell an employer why you think you're suitable for a particular job • *I've read Joe's personal statement, and he sounds an ideal candidate.*

training VERB
to learn the skills that you need in order to do something • *Stephen is training to be a teacher.*

Unit 14

bring VERB
to have someone or something with you when you come to a place • *Remember to bring some money.*

connected ADJECTIVE
used for describing a relationship between things • *She described the problems connected with a high-fat diet.*

eastern ADJECTIVE
in or from the east of a place • *...Eastern Europe.*

equal VERB
to be the same as a particular number or amount
• *9 minus 7 equals 2.*

loan NOUN
an amount of money that you borrow • *Right now it's very difficult to get a loan from a bank.*

summarise VERB
to give a brief description of the main points of something • *The story can be summarised in three sentences.*

symbol NOUN
a number, a letter or a shape that represents a particular thing • *The chemical symbol for Carbon is 'C'.*

Unit 15

affect VERB
to cause someone or something to change in some way • *This problem affects all of us.*

apologise VERB
to say that you are sorry • *He apologised to everyone.*

catch up VERB
to reach the same level as someone else • *You'll have to work hard to catch up.*

miss VERB
to not take part in a meeting or an activity • *He missed the party because he had to work.*

polite ADJECTIVE
behaving with respect towards other people • *He seemed a quiet and very polite young man.*

problem NOUN
something or someone that causes difficulties
• *Pollution is a problem in this city.*

solution NOUN
a way of dealing with a problem • *They both want to find a solution to the conflict.*

take a day off PHRASE to have a day away from work or school • *She took the day off as she felt ill.*

Unit 16

construction NOUN
the building of things such as houses, roads and bridges • *The new bridge is under construction.*

experience NOUN
knowledge or skill in a job or activity that you have

done for a long time • *No teaching experience is necessary for this job.*

industry NOUN
the work of making things in factories • *The meeting was for leaders in banking and industry.*

musical ADJECTIVE
having a natural ability and interest in music • *I come from a musical family.*

networking NOUN
trying to meet new people who might be useful to you in your job or career • *I did a bit of networking at the conference.*

opportunities NOUN
situations in which it is possible for you to do things that you want to do • *Young people need more opportunities to find employment.*

personal ADJECTIVE
relating to a particular person • *The story is based on his own personal experience.*

project manager NOUN
a person in a company who plans and organises pieces of work • *The project manager is responsible for completing the job on time.*

Unit 17

blog NOUN
a website that describes the daily life of the person who writes it, and also their thoughts and ideas
• *His blog was later published as a book.* VERB to write regularly about your daily life, thoughts and ideas, on a website • *She blogs about politics on her website.*

building NOUN
a structure that has a roof and walls • *They lived on the top floor of the building.*

countryside NOUN
land that is away from cities and towns • *I've always loved the English countryside.*

cycle VERB
to ride a bicycle • *He cycles to school every day.*

popular ADJECTIVE
liked by a lot of people • *Chocolate sauce is always popular with children.*

probably ADVERB
likely to be true or to happen, although you are not sure • *I will probably go home on Tuesday.*

reindeer NOUN
a big animal with large horns that lives in northern areas of Europe, Asia and America • *A herd of reindeer was seen in the forest.*

traffic NOUN

all the vehicles that are on a particular road at one time • *There was heavy traffic on the roads.*

Unit 18

adopt VERB

to take someone else's child into your own family and make them legally your son or daughter • *There are hundreds of people who want to adopt a child.*

character NOUN

a letter, number, or other symbol that is written or printed • *I could not read the Chinese characters.*

concert NOUN

a performance of music • *The weekend began with an outdoor rock concert.*

by mistake PHRASE accidentally • *I was in a hurry and called the wrong number by mistake.*

share VERB

to make something available to other people on a social networking website • *I shared the link to the story so others could read it.*

timeline NOUN

a sequence of messages shown on a social networking website • *The timeline showed me all the messages sent to me last week.*

tornado NOUN

a storm with strong winds that spin around very fast and cause a lot of damage • *The tornado destroyed many buildings in the town.*

traffic jam NOUN

a long line of vehicles that cannot move forward, or can only move very slowly • *The accident caused a huge traffic jam.*

Unit 19

caption NOUN

a piece of writing next to a picture, that tells you something about the picture • *The photo had the caption 'John, aged 6 years'.*

close down VERB

to stop all work in a place, usually for ever • *I'm sad that I've had to close down my shop!*

graduation NOUN

a special ceremony for students when they have completed their studies at a university or college • *Her parents came to her graduation.*

post VERB

to put information on a website so that other people can see it • *The statement was posted on the Internet.*

profile NOUN

your personal information on a social networking website • *I need to update my profile with my new telephone number.*

serious ADJECTIVE

important and deserving of thoughtful consideration • *This is a very serious problem.* sincere about what you are saying, doing or intending to do • *You really are serious about this, aren't you?*

spare ADJECTIVE

used for describing extra things that you keep in case you need them • *I have a spare pen if you need one.*

style NOUN

the way in which something is done • *I prefer the Indian style of cooking.*

result NOUN

something that happens or exists because something else has happened • *People developed the disease as a direct result of their work.*

Unit 20

diner NOUN

a small cheap restaurant that is open all day • *After leaving the party last night, we went to a diner to eat.*

hostel NOUN

a large house where people can stay cheaply for a short time • *I will be staying in a hostel when I travel to Milan.*

modify VERB

to change something slightly, usually in order to improve it • *Helen and her husband modified the design of the house to suit their family's needs.*

rude ADJECTIVE

not polite • *He's so rude to her friends.*

service NOUN

the help that people in a restaurant or a shop give you • *We always receive good service in that restaurant.*

staff NOUN

the people who work for an organization • *The hospital staff were very good.*

terrible ADJECTIVE

extremely bad • *I have a terrible singing voice.*

ANSWER KEY

Unit 1   Short emails

Looking closely

1

1   Lewis wants Julie to come to a comedy show and dinner at a Thai restaurant on Thursday night.

2   Julie wants to go to an Italian restaurant.

3   Yes, Julie does like comedy.

4   No, Julie does not like Thai food. She prefers Italian food.

Language focus

1

1 O	3 P	5 P	7 O
2 C	4 C	6 P	

2

1   Let's go to the cinema on Wednesday?

2   We could play football?

3   How about going to an Italian restaurant?

4   Why don't we go and see some comedy?

5   Would you like to go to the park after work tomorrow?

Writing clearly

1

Sample answers:

1   No thanks, I'm busy then.

2   Yes, that sounds like fun.

3   OK, let's do it!

4   Thanks, but I have other plans.

5   I'd love to!

2

Sample answers:

1   a   Why don't we go to the cinema on Saturday?

    b   Sorry, I'm busy then.

    c   No thanks, I'm busy on Saturday. Why don't we go on Sunday instead?

2   a   Why don't we go to a Chinese restaurant on Monday?

    b   I'd love to go out for dinner, but why don't we go to a Japanese restaurant instead?

Language focus

1

The first email is informal, the second email is formal.

2

Sample answers:

1   Hi/Hey ...I...

2   Dear ...F...

3   What's up? ...I...

4   I hope you are well. ...F...

5   Speak soon./See you soon. ...I...

6   Love/Hugs/Kisses ...I..

7   Kind regards ...F...

8   x (= kiss) ...I...

9   Cheers. ..I...

10   I look forward to hearing from you. ...F...

Writing clearly

1

Sample answers:

1   Hey Frida..... Speak soon, hugs, Kx

2   Hi Dad. How're you? ... love, Petra xx

3   Hi Sunil, how's it going? ... Cheers, Iain

4   Dear National Bank ... Kind regards, Anastasia

2

Hey Janet,

How are you? If you're free tomorrow, would you like to go to the cinema? There's a nice new Italian place by the river. Maybe we could try it? Let me know if you want to go.

xx

Carrie

Get writing

1

Sample answer:

Hi Xiao Li

Great to see you again last week. What are you up to next Thursday evening? There's a new play at the Young Vic theatre and I've got an extra ticket. Later we could go to eat at the new Spanish place on York Road if you like – yum!

Let me know if you're free.

Hugs!

Mauricio x

2

Sample answer:

Dear Mr Allen

I hope you are well.

Are you available next Saturday for a lesson? I would like to meet at 2 p.m. at my house, 31a Camberwell Grove.

I look forward to hearing from you.

Kind regards

Miguel

Unit 2   Longer emails

Looking closely

1

1   Stan is sending the email. Aleks is receiving the email.

2   Aleks is Stan's younger brother.

3   In Toronto Stan lived at home with his family. In Edinburgh he shares a flat with two classmates. In Edinburgh he goes to university each day, eats sausages and sandwiches, goes out with his classmates and works in an Italian restaurant. In Edinburgh he cleans and does the dishes. He thinks Edinburgh is smaller and colder than Toronto.

Language focus

1

	Stan's daily routine in Edinburgh
Morning	gets up around 7.30, walks to university, buys breakfast in a local café, eats sausages for breakfast, has classes all morning
Afternoon	eats lunch in the canteen with his classmates, studies or goes for a walk around town
Evening	goes out with his classmates
Fri/Sat evening	washes dishes in an Italian restaurant

2

1   I eat lunch at 1.00 p.m.

2   I always get up at 8.00 a.m.

3   I work from 9 to 5.

4   In the afternoon I go to the gym.

5   In the evening I work at the cinema.

6   In the evening I study or watch TV.

3

1   walks   3   go out   5   has

2   eat   4   have

4

Sample answers:

	Your daily activities	**Your friend's daily activities**
Mornings	I get up at 7.00a.m. I brush my teeth. I make coffee and eat cereal for breakfast. I go to school.	She gets up at 8.00 a.m. She eats breakfast at her local café. She goes to work.
Afternoons	I eat lunch in the school canteen with my friends. I study.	She eats sandwiches at work. She works all afternoon and then goes to the gym.
Evenings	I make dinner and watch TV. Sometimes I go for a walk.	She goes out with her friends.
Weekends	I go to the gym. I go for a walk in the park.	She goes to the cinema and watches TV.

Language focus

5

1   a   2   c   3   b

6

Sample answer:

Hi Mum.

Thanks for sending me the books – they look really interesting!

I'm having a lovely time here in Granada. The weather is beautiful and Spanish people are very friendly. Learning Spanish is easy, because no one wants to speak English!

Let me tell you about a typical day here. I get up at 9 a.m. and have coffee and pastries for breakfast. Then Inés, my Spanish teacher, comes to my house and gives me a lesson. For lunch I go to a café in the square near my apartment. Then I have a siesta – that's the part of the afternoon when Spanish people relax or sleep. Most of the shops close for a few hours. In the evening I meet my friend Jorge and we talk or go for a walk. We sometimes go out for tapas. Spanish people eat dinner very late. Sometimes I don't get home until 1 a.m.!

You and Dad must come and visit me here. You can stay with Jorge's parents. I'll even teach you some Spanish!

All my love

Lisbeth

Writing clearly

1

Sample answers:

1   Hope you're well. It's lovely here!

2   Every morning I get up around 8.30 a.m. I have breakfast and walk to work. I buy a coffee at my local café.

3   My friend Tom is always busy. He gets up at 6.00 a.m. and goes to the gym. Then he has breakfast and goes to university. He studies all day from 9.00 a.m. to 5.00 a.m. Then he works in a local restaurant in the evenings.

4   I miss you! Write to me soon.

Language focus

1

1   I miss you./I miss you!

2   Every day I go to the gym.

3   Can you believe I've been in Rio for two months now?

4   Often Peter, my friend, goes fishing.

5   I love Paris – it's amazing!

Get writing

1

Sample answer:

Hi Dad

It's so great here in Hong Kong – I wish you could see it!

Let me tell you about my daily routine. In the mornings I get up around 8.00 a.m. and walk to my local café for a coffee and breakfast. I take the bus to my office and start work at 9.30 a.m. In the afternoons I eat lunch with my colleagues. Sometimes we have noodles, or sometimes I have a sandwich. After work I go out with my colleagues. We eat dinner in lots of different restaurants – the food here is amazing!

Life here is so different to life at home. It's so hot, and I miss you and Mum. But I'm having a really great time!

Give Mum my love. I miss you both!

Love

Sam x

Unit 3   Postcards

Looking closely

1

1   The postcard is from Rosie.

2   The postcard is to Jo, Phillip, Kristine & Lee (who are probably Rosie's flatmates).

3   Rosie mentions going to see the pyramids, taking photos, riding a camel, walking around Cairo and eating some delicious food.

4   She is going to take a cruise down the Nile.

2

1 greeting	3 signature	5 address
2 message	4 stamp	6 P.S.

Language focus

1

1	T	5	F	9	P
2	P	6	P	10	P
3	T	7	T		
4	F	8	T		

2

Hi Misty

I'm having a <u>great time</u> in Rome – the <u>weather is</u> amazing!

Yesterday I <u>went to see</u> the Trevi fountain. It was really beautiful. In the evening I found a lovely little restaurant and <u>ate</u> too much pizza!

Tomorrow I'm <u>going to</u> visit the Vatican.

<u>Wish you were here! See you</u> soon!

Love, Trev

P.S. I bought you a lovely present!

3

Dear Guy, Jackie and Mia

We are having a wonderful time in Hong Kong.

Yesterday we <u>took</u> the Star Ferry to Tsim Sha Tsui and <u>went</u> shopping. I <u>bought</u> a jade necklace and Papa <u>bought</u> a silk shirt. Last night we <u>ate</u> in a tiny restaurant - the food <u>was</u> delicious!

Tomorrow we're going to visit Happy Valley to watch the horse racing. Then we're going to eat dim sum.

We miss you!

lots of love

Mama and Papa xx

4

1 c   2 a   3 d   4 b   5 e

5

1 We <u>ate</u> noodles at a Japanese restaurant.

2 Patrick <u>climbed</u> the mountain and <u>saw</u> a snake.

3 We <u>visited</u> the British Museum and <u>saw</u> the exhibition.

4 I <u>took</u> a bus to <u>visit</u> the Tower of London.

5 Yesterday I <u>went</u> to the market and <u>bought</u> a silk scarf.

6

1 We're going to eat at a French restaurant.

2 I'm going to go to the cinema this evening./We're going to the cinema this evening.

3 I think I'm going to like Cairo.

4 We're going to visit the museum tomorrow.

Get writing

1

Sample answers:

1 I took the bus to Buckingham Palace – it was amazing!

2 Yesterday I went to a French restaurant – the food was delicious!

3 Today I'm going shopping.

4 Tomorrow I'm going to visit the British Museum.

2

Sample answer:

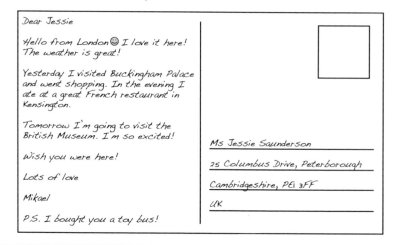

Dear Jessie

Hello from London☺ I love it here! The weather is great!

Yesterday I visited Buckingham Palace and went shopping. In the evening I ate at a great French restaurant in Kensington.

Tomorrow I'm going to visit the British Museum. I'm so excited!

Wish you were here!

Lots of love

Mikael

P.S. I bought you a toy bus!

Ms Jessie Saunderson

25 Columbus Drive, Peterborough

Cambridgeshire, PE1 3FF

UK

Unit 4   Text messages

Looking closely

1

1 Joanne is at a restaurant.

2 She is too early.

3 Dee will come to the restaurant in 15 minutes.

2

1 g   3 d   5 f   7 c

2 a   4 b   6 e

Language focus

1

Why don't u order now?

2

1 Why don't we go to the cinema instead?

2 Shall we watch another film?

3 Let's go to a Japanese restaurant instead.

4 How about playing tennis on Wednesday?

3

Sample answers:

1 Why don't we go to a Spanish restaurant instead?

2 Let's go to the cinema instead.

3 Why don't we go to the gym instead?

4 How about staying at home instead?

5 Shall we go and see some comedy instead?

Looking closely

1

1 Do you still want to play tennis?

2 I want to play tennis… What should we do instead?

3 I hate the gym!

4 Maybe we could stay in and watch football instead?

5 Great! I'll order pizza.

6 Thanks. I'll see you later!

2

Sample answers:

1 U got any food 4 dinner?

2 Can't come out 2nite. 2 busy.

3 Sorry. Thought we were meeting at 9.

4 U want 2 go 2 gym 2nite?

5 gr8! Want me 2 bring something to drink?

Language focus

1

1	in	3	at/in	5	at
2	at/in	4	at		

Get writing

1

Sample answers:

1 Do u want 2 go 2 the cinema 2nite?

2 Why don't we go 2 the Italian restaurant this weekend?

3 Let's go 2 the park and play tennis.

2

Sample answers:

1 Oh no! Let's go 2 c some comedy instead.

2 OK. Why don't we go 2 the Japanese restaurant instead?

3 How about going 2 the gym?

Unit 5   Sharing news online

Looking closely

1

1 Elodie wants Pete to go out after work.

2 Pete can't because he has lots of work to do.

3 Pete agrees to come out later, for dinner.

2

1 S   2 S   3 SO   4 O   5 S

Language focus

1

Kerry

Hey Phil, my boss says I **1** <u>have to</u> work late today. :(I don't think I can come to the party – sorry!

Phil

But you **2** <u>have to</u> come! It won't be any fun without you!

Kerry

But everyone else in my office **3** <u>has to</u> work late. They'll be angry if I get to leave early.

Phil

I think you **4** <u>should</u> talk to your boss. Tell her this is important.

Kerry

What do you think I **5** <u>should</u> say?

Phil

Tell her it's your brother's birthday party and you **6** <u>have</u> to go.

Kerry

You're right. I **7** <u>should</u> stand up for myself. Wish me luck!

2

1	mustn't	4	mustn't
2	don't have to	5	doesn't have to
3	don't have to		

3

You won't believe this, but

Keira told me

She also said that

I've got some news too

Writing clearly

1

Sample answers:

1 Did you know that I have a new job?

2 You won't believe this but Bob and Evie are getting married!

3 I've got some news. I didn't get the job I wanted.

4 I've got some exciting news. I'm moving to Colombia!

5 Alex told me that he lost his job.

Sample answers:

1 Really? That's great!

2 OMG! Wow!

3 Really! I'm sorry to hear that.

4 Wow! That's amazing!

5 OMG! That's terrible.

Language focus

1

Sample answers:

1 Oh, that's nice. Sorry, but I've got to go now. Let's talk again soon.

2 Really? I'm sorry to hear that. It was nice chatting to you, but I'm afraid I have to go.

3 I'm good, thanks. I'd love to talk more, but I have to go.

Get writing

1

Sample answers:

1 Hi. I'm fine. Yes, I can talk.

2 Really? Wow! That's great!

3 Oh no! That's terrible!

4 OK.

5 No problem. Speak soon.

2

Sample answers:

1 Hey Misty. How are you? Can you talk?

2 You won't believe this, but I've got a new job!

Unit 6   Filling in forms

Looking closely

1

doctor's surgery, school / college, library, gym, dentist, bank, work

2

1 Leila

2 Woman

3 She is registering as a new patient at the Fairside GP Clinic.

3

Language focus

1

Students' own answers.

2

Students' own answers.

Looking closely

1

1 S Phillips

2 Samuel Phillips

3 12th April 2013

4 Promise

Fairside GP Clinic
New Patient Registration Form

Personal information Title: (Miss)/Ms/Mrs/Mr Gender: M/(F)   Date of Birth: |_|4| |0|4| |8|9|
DD   MM   YY

First Name: |L|E|I|L|A| |_|_|_|...
Middle Name: |A|N|N|E| |_|_|_|...
Last Name: |W|A|T|S|O|N| |_|_|_|...
Primary language: _English_   Nationality: _British_   Marital status: (single)/married

Contact information Home Address:

House/Flat no: |_|4|_|_| Street: |H|A|D|E|N| |S|T|R|E|E|T| |_|_|...
Town/City: |L|E|E|D|S| |_|_|_|...| Postcode: |L|2| |3| |S|D| |_|_|_|
Email address: |L|.|W|A|T|S|O|N|@|L|E|E|D|S|.|A|C|.|O|R|G| |_|_|...
Home tel: _0113 343 786_   Mobile tel: _097865643321_

Language focus

1

Students' own answers.

Personal details:

Title: _Miss_   Last name: Clarke

First name: _Lucie_

DOB: _05_ / _07_ / _1986_   Gender: _Female_ Marital status: _Single_

Contact details:

House number: _27_   Street: _Park Place_

Town: _Bristol_   Postcode: _BR3 2XF_ Email address: _l.clarke@freemail.org_

Get writing

1

2

Students' own answers.

Unit 7   'To do' lists

Looking closely

1

1	Buy	4	Tidy	7	Meet
2	Send	5	Answer		
3	Pick up	6	Read		

2

1 The first list is for everyday tasks like shopping and cleaning. The second list is for work tasks.

2 The first list is handwritten. The second is written on a computer. The writer of the first list draws a line through tasks he/she has completed. The writer of the second list ticks tasks he/she has completed.

3 The writer of the first list has taken their car to the garage.

4 The writer of the second list hasn't met Jessie and Phil for lunch or tidied his/her desk.

Language focus

1

1	Meet	5	Make	9	Do
2	Pick up	6	Go to	10	Buy
3	Tidy	7	Write		
4	Read	8	Call		

2

1 Visit <u>the</u> supermarket <u>and</u> buy <u>some</u> eggs

2 <u>Please</u> pick up <u>the</u> dry cleaning.

3 Call Michaela, about <u>the</u> party.

4 Read <u>the</u> report <u>and</u> make notes <u>on</u> it.

5 Buy Max <u>a</u> birthday card <u>and</u> send it.

3

1 Please make <u>the/some</u> coffee before <u>the</u> meeting.

2 Buy cereal at <u>the</u> supermarket.

3 Pick up <u>the</u> dry cleaning when you are in town.

4 Go to the meeting <u>on</u> Thursday.

5 Send the email <u>to</u> Jane.

6 <u>The</u> meeting starts <u>at</u> 11.30 a.m.

7 Take <u>some</u> notes when you are in <u>the</u> meeting.

8 Do <u>the</u> washing up and tidy <u>the</u> house.

Writing clearly

1

Sample answers:

1 Visit supermarket. Buy eggs.

2 Pick up dry cleaning.

3 Call Michaela about party

4 Read report. Make notes.

5 Buy Max birthday card. Send it.

2

Sample answers:

1   Tidy house.
2   Take car to garage.
3   Call Bradley this afternoon.
4   At meeting: make coffee, take notes.
5   Buy eggs, cereal, pizza at supermarket.

Looking closely

1

1   Buying a gift for Sandra (we know because there are two asterisks ** in front of it).
2   Buying a new dress for the party (we know because there is one asterisk * in front of it).
3   Getting her shoes fixed (we know because she has drawn a wavy line through it).
4   Buying a card (we know because she has used a question mark).
5   She has bought a gift for Sandra and met Joe and Alix for lunch (we know because she has ticked these tasks).

Get writing

1

Sample answer:

- Go to shopping centre:
  - buy gift for Sandra
  - buy new dress
  - buy wrapping paper for gift
  - buy card?
- Meet Joe & Alix for lunch 12.30.

2

Sample answers:

1   My to do list for this week:
  - Take car to garage
  - Tidy house
  - Buy birthday gift for Dad
  - Go to supermarket.
2   My to do list for school:
  - Do homework:
    - Answer questions on pages 3-4
    - Read about imperatives
    - Learn 10 new verbs
  - Meet Ciara and Jose for lunch on Wednesday.
  - Talk to teacher about homework on Thursday.
  - Buy new pens.

Unit 8   Invitations and directions

Looking closely

1

1   It is a surprise party. This means that Marie doesn't know about the party.
2   Arrive between 7 and 7.30pm. Don't tell Marie about the party.
3   Sam Rogers, the General Manager of the company where James works.
4   Give some money for his leaving gift.

Language focus

1

1   Please join us at our wedding celebration.
2   You are invited to Louise's birthday party.
3   We are having an engagement party.
4   I'm having a leaving party.
5   Please join me at my 30th birthday party.
6   I'm having a dinner party on 29th November. Please come.

2

1	invited	4	married
2	invitation	5	housewarming
3	birthday		

3

1	c	3	e	5	d
2	a	4	b		

4

1	christening	4	engagement
2	funeral	5	housewarming
3	retirement		

Writing clearly

1

Sample answers:

1   I'm having a party for my 19th birthday.
2   Please join us at a surprise birthday party for Joanna.
3   You are invited to Jen's leaving party next Friday.
4   Please come to a surprise retirement party for Sally. Don't tell her about it!

Language focus

1

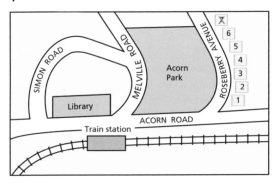

Get writing

1

1 Go left along Elm Row and turn left onto Park Street. Number 7 is opposite the library.

2 Cross the street and turn left. Turn right onto Dale Street. Number 5 is on the right.

3 Turn left and go straight along Elm Row. Turn left onto Park Street, then turn left again along London Road. The Pizzeria is on the left, after the bridge.

2

Sample answer:

You are invited to Kirsten's 34th birthday party on Wednesday, 4th October.

The party will be at King's Bowling Alley, Leyton Road, from 7.30pm.

3

Sample answer:

To: my friends

From: Simon

Subject: Housewarming party

Hi Everyone

We're having a housewarming party this Friday from 7pm. Please come and bring some food to share.

Our address is 17a Cumberland Drive. From the train station go straight along Hillside Avenue, turn left onto Sutton Road then left again onto Cumberland Drive. Our house is opposite the park.

See you on Friday!

Simon

Unit 9   Advertising a room

Looking closely

1

1 Angie and Marie are renting out the room.

2 A friendly student or a young professional (someone with a job).

3 The room is fully-furnished, bright and comfortable.

4 Approximately £1327.00 (£412 deposit + £915 rent)

2

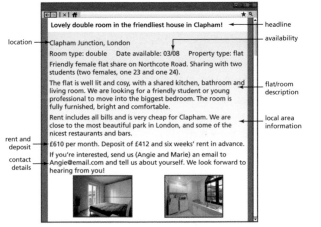

Language focus

1

The advert does not say what the local area is like.

2

1	house	4	housemate
2	single	5	fully furnished
3	23	6	deposit

3

1	f	3	a	5	e
2	d	4	c	6	b

Language focus

1

First advert: friendliest, biggest, the most beautiful, the nicest

Second advert: the cheapest, the nicest

2

1	the cosiest	4	the most attractive
2	the most comfortable	5	the cheapest
3	the nicest	6	the prettiest

3

1   Our flat is the cheapest in London.

2   The room is the most comfortable in the house.

3   The room has the best view of the park.

4   Our local area has the nicest restaurants in Birmingham.

5   The most attractive parks in London are near our house.

Get writing

1

Sample answers:

1   My local area has the most beautiful park in Bristol.

2   The rent is the cheapest in my local area.

3   Our local area has the most interesting buildings in Liverpool.

4   My room has the prettiest view I have seen.

5   This is the lightest room in the house.

6   My room is the warmest room in the house.

7   Our local area has the best restaurants.

2

Sample answer:

Beautiful room available in Clifton area of Bristol.

Fully-furnished double room available in a two-bedroomed flat in Clifton, sharing with a 22-year-old female student. The room is very nice, and has the loveliest view in the house.

The local area is very nice and has lots of great restaurants.

Rent is £650 per month, including bills. Deposit is £800.

Email Natalie@newmail.org if you want to know more.

3

Students' own answers.

Unit 10   Giving and getting advice

Looking closely

1

1   No. Lilian used to live in Shanghai. Duane is moving there soon.

2   No. Duane is a vegetarian (he doesn't eat any kind of meat).

3   Probably not (Lilian tells him to learn some Mandarin before he goes to Shanghai).

2

1   Puxi

2   Vegetarian House on Wukang Road

3   Learn some Mandarin, take the ferry across the Huang Pu River at night.

Language focus

1

Asking for advice: I'd really like your advice. Where do you think I should…? What are some…? Any other advice?

2

1   Where do you think I should live?

2   What restaurants should I eat at?

3   What are some good places to visit?

4   Where do you think I should look for an apartment?

5   What museums would you recommend?

3

1   I think you'd like living/to live in Pudong.

2   I recommend that you eat at the Happy Duck restaurant.

3   You have to try the food at Chinese Kitchen.

4   You should learn some Mandarin before you go to China.

Language focus

1

Food	Transport	Culture
café, restaurant	metro, taxi, bus, ferry	museum, theatre, art gallery

2

1   theatre   4   taxi   7   restaurant

2   café   5   museum   8   art gallery

3   ferry   6   metro   9   bus

3

What to eat and drink:

Seafood at the Crispy Crab on Louisburg Square

Coffee at the café in the market on Clinton Street

How to travel:

Walk along the Freedom Trail and the Charles River

Take a bus or taxi if tired

Take the ferry to the Boston Harbor Islands

What to see:

The Freedom Trail

The Boston Harbor Islands

The Charles River

Get writing

1

Sample answer:

Hi Sarah

I hope you are well.

I have some exciting news: I'm moving to San Francisco! I've got a new job there and I start in three weeks!

I know you lived in San Francisco for a long time. I'd really like your advice. Where do you think I should live? Are there any nice, cheap parts of the city?

Can you recommend any good restaurants? I love Chinese food and I know there is a big Chinatown in San Francisco. Also, what's the best way to travel around? Any other advice?

Thanks for helping me out.

Speak soon

Marta

2

Sample answer:

Hey Gerard

Congratulations on your new job. Cologne is an amazing city. I'm sure you will love it there!

I recommend that you find a place to live near the centre. That way you can walk to work easily. There are lots of great restaurants to try. I suggest you eat at Haxenhaus on Salzgasse – that was my favourite restaurant. Also, you have to visit the cathedral – it really is the most beautiful cathedral in Germany!

The best way to travel around is to walk, but you can also take a bus or a train if you want.

Good luck and send me an email soon!

Love, Lisbeth

Unit 11   Course applications

Looking closely

1

1   By herself (using self-study books, CDs and films) and while travelling in Spain.
2   A Spanish language school.
3   She wants to study French and Spanish at University, then to live and work in South America.

2

Things Alison has done in the past	Things Alison wants to do in the future
Got an A in her French exam; travelled for six weeks in France, Spain and Italy (studied all three languages); studied Spanish to Intermediate level; watched many Spanish films.	Study Spanish at Insitituto de España in Manchester; study French and Spanish at University; live and work in South America.

Language focus

1

Sentences in the past simple tense:
Last year I got an A in my French exam. In 2012 I travelled for six weeks in France, Spain and Italy and practised speaking all three languages.

2

Sentences in the present perfect tense:
I have studied Spanish to Intermediate level using self-study books and CDs and I have also watched many Spanish films.

Alison has used the present perfect tense because she wants to talk about past achievements she is still working on.

3

1 have	3 has	5 has
2 has	4 have	

4

1   I lived in Norway for three years.
2   Sasha studied Portuguese for several months.
3   Alan travelled in Asia and Africa.
4   I enjoyed learning about Chinese history.
5   In Chile, I studied Spanish and Business.

Writing clearly

1

Completed achievements	Achievements Miguel is still working on
Studied at First School of English, London in 2008. Got a Grade B in his FCE in 2008. Worked as an admin assistant at Aquinas Office Tech in Madrid in 2011. Got a degree in Computer Sciences and Maths, Technical University of Madrid.	A two-month placement at En-path Computer Software Ltd (he will finish in June).

2

1 studied	4 have completed
2 passed	5 working
3 worked	

Language focus

1

Students' own answers.

Get writing

1

Describe your qualifications and experience.

I took a course in Japanese at the Nippon School in Frankfurt. I passed with an A. From 2009–2012 I studied German, English and History at my school in Frankfurt. I got an A in all these subjects.

During summer 2011 I worked as a waiter in a small restaurant. Since 2012, I have worked as an admin assistant in a language school.

What are your plans for the future?

My goal is to study Japanese and to live and work in Japan. In three years' time I plan to be living in Tokyo and studying Japanese. My greatest ambition is to be fluent in Japanese.

2

Sample answer:

I graduated with a first class honours degree in Fine Art from Goldsmiths University in London in 2012. At school, I studied Art, History and English. I got As in each subject. Every summer since 2009 I have worked as a receptionist in the art gallery in my home town.

3

Sample answer:

I would like to work as a painter. My goal is to take an MA in Fine Art at the Royal College of Art. One day I hope to be a really good painter.

Unit 12   Asking for help

Looking closely

1

1   They are probably classmates who study English together.

2   Alexis is confused about the present continuous tense.

3   Samira adds Mike to the conversation to help Alexis.

4   Mike looks for his notes to help Alexis remember what happened in class.

2

1	A	3	RN	5	RP	7	RP	9	A
2	A	4	RN	6	A	8	A	10	RP

Language focus

1

'Wh' questions in the past simple: What did the teacher say about it? What part didn't you understand? How did the teacher explain it? ('How' is not a 'wh' question word, but it works in the same way.)

These questions all contain the verb 'to do'.

2

1	What	3	Which	5	Which
2	When	4	What	6	Why

3

1   What/Which

2   What/Which

3   How/When/Where

4   When/Where/What

5   How/When/Where

6   Who

Language focus

1

1   Do you remember what we did yesterday?

2   Can you help me with my homework?

3   Do you remember what the teacher said?

4   What did the teacher say about adjectives?

5   Did you understand our lesson yesterday?

6   Can you explain what 'infinitive' means?

2

1   Did you understand what she said yesterday?

2   What did the teacher say about main verbs?

3   Can you explain what 'modal' means? I don't understand.

4   I didn't understand the lesson. Can you explain it to me?

3

Sample answers:

1   Sorry, I can't remember either.

2   Let me explain …

3   The teacher said that …

4   Let me explain …

5   Yes, what didn't you understand?

6   Of course. An 'Infinitive' is …

Get writing

1

1   What did the teacher say about modal verbs?

2   When did (the teacher say that) we have to hand in our homework?

3 Where did the teacher say our exam is/was next week?

4 How did you answer the questions in the book?

2

Suggested answers:

1 Did you understand our English class yesterday?

2 What did she say about how to form it/the present perfect tense?

3 When did she say we have to hand in our homework?

3

Suggested answers:

1 No, sorry. I didn't understand it either.

2 I really don't know.

3 Sorry. I can't remember!

Unit 13 Job applications

Looking closely

1

1 part-time

2 You must have a neat appearance and be friendly.

3 It is useful if you have worked in a shop before, know how to serve customers, keep the shop tidy and use a till. It is also useful if you can speak a foreign language.

4 The company will provide training.

2

1 d   3 e   5 c
2 b   4 a

3

Do they have ......

1 experience? (yes)

2 a neat appearance? (yes)

3 a friendly personality? (yes)

Can they …

1 start immediately? (no)

2 speak any foreign languages? (yes)

3 take payments? (yes)

4

1 d   3 b   5 c
2 f   4 e   6 a

5

1 experienced   5 using
2 waiter   6 tidy
3 friendly   7 goal
4 serving   8 degree

Looking closely

1

	Angus	Megan
Work experience in a shop	Yes. Worked as shop assistant at Comfy Sofas.	No
Other work experience	Yes. Has worked as a waiter.	Yes. Has worked in restaurants and in an office.
Languages	English, French and some German	English
Immediate start?	no	yes
Other notes	Business student	Fashion Design student, loves fashion, can provide references

Angus has more experience and can speak more languages than Megan, but Megan is working in Fashion so may be more suitable. Either Angus or Megan could get offered the job.

Get writing

2

Sample answer:

I am a friendly, confident reliable person. I have worked in restaurants and in an office as an admin assistant. I can serve customers and use a till. I love fashion and am studying Fashion Design. My goal is to be a fashion designer and I want to get a part-time job in a clothes shop while I am studying.

2-4 Own answers

Unit 14 Taking notes

Looking closely

1

1 The lecture is about the history of the English language.

2 The writer summarises long sentences, shortens words and uses symbols.

3 Yes.

2

1 c	3 e	5 b
2 a	4 f	6 d

Language focus

1

Symbols:

+

→

C

=

K

2

Sample answers:

1   German and French are connected to English.
2   Three plus seven equals ten.
3   In the past British people spoke Brythonic or Latin.
4   There are Hindi and Arabic words in English.
5   Angles and Romans are connected to British people.
6   Five plus three does not equal nine.
7   'Difficult' does not mean the same as 'bad'.
8   'Glad' means 'happy'.

3

1   Chinese ≠ English.
2   8 + 10 ≠ 20
3   Old Norse → English
4   At school we can study English + History / English + German

Looking closely

1

1   Eastern parts of Britain, 5th Century ·
2   Eastern parts of Britain
3   taught/brought; to British people/to Britain
4   moved to/came to; taught their language/began to learn

2

Students' own answers.

3

Sample answers:

1   In the 11th Century, the Normans brought Old Norman to Britain and taught it to British people.
2   New words (such as 'social media' and 'Tweeting') are added to English every year.

Language focus

1

1   Table for 2 – 8p.m.
2   For meeting get 2 white teas, one black coffee, two white coffees.
3   After meeting Jenny call Bob, Nick write report for Sara.
4   Collins English Dictionary. Buy 3 copies.
5   Email Chris and Phil about meeting next Tuesday.

Get writing

1

Sample answers:

1

A: thinks we shd. move out of office because too exp.

S: Disagrees. Everyone happy here. Moving offices exp. too.

A & S: We shd. email M.

2

1 x cheese and tom. Pizza

Deliver to 25 Armagh Rd.

2

English is difficult to learn. Why?

1. Spelling

No simple way 2 write Eng. sounds = Eng. words hard to spell

Hard to guess sp. from pron + hard to guess pron. from sp.

2. Homophones

Eng. has lots of homophones → Eng. hard.

H = words that sound the same but diff. sp. & meaning, e.g. they're/there

---

Unit 15   Problems at work or school

Looking closely

1

1   Sarbjit is unwell (ill) and needs to take a day off work. Kassia's mother was unwell and so she had to miss two lessons.

2   Sarbjit suggests taking a sick day (a day off work). If he is still sick tomorrow he says he will work at home. Kassia suggests 'catching up' on the work she has missed (i.e. she will do the work late). She asks if she can do any of the exercises in her textbook to help her catch up.

2

1 DP	3 SS	5 SS	7 SS
2 DP	4 SS	6 DP	8 SS

Language focus

1

1 Sorry about not doing my homework.
2 I apologise for forgetting to send the email.
3 I'm afraid that I can't come to work today.
4 I'm sorry that I have to take a day off work.
5 I apologise for missing class on Friday.

2

Sample answers:

1 I'm sorry that I forgot to call you yesterday.
2 I apologise that I couldn't go to my English classes last week.
3 I'm afraid that I forgot to do my homework.
4 Sorry I didn't have time to send that email to you.
5 I'm sorry I was late for work again.

Language focus

3

1 Sentences in the first conditional: If I'm still sick tomorrow, I will work from home. You can call me if you need to ask any questions about work.
2 The problem in the first sentence = he might be sick (ill) tomorrow. The problem in the second sentence = Sarbjit's boss might need to ask Sarbjit some questions (but Sarbjit will be at home).
3 The solution in the first sentence = Sarbjit will work from (at) home. The solution in the second sentence = Sarbjit's boss can call him on the telephone.

4

1 If	3 will	5 I
2 I'll	4 if	

5

Sample answers:

1 If I don't come to work tomorrow, I'll work late the next day.
2 If I don't pass my English test, I will take it again.

3 I'll do extra work if my teacher says I should.
4 I will come to work early if my boss needs me to.

Looking closely

1

1 The second email is more polite.
2 I'm sorry that…, I'm afraid…, as soon as possible, Please let me know what you'd like me to do, Kind regards

2

Sample answers:

1 I'm sorry that I didn't have time to give you my report yesterday.
2 Please let me know what you'd like me to do.
3 I'm afraid that I didn't have time to finish my other work.
4 I'm sorry that I'm too busy to write the report today. I will try to write it tomorrow.

Get writing

1

Sample answer:

Dear Mr Potts

I'm sorry, but I need some extra time to complete my homework this week. I have to work late every night this week, and my boss won't let me take any time off.

If you give me some more time, I will make sure I hand in my homework on Monday morning.

Thanks for your help!

Kind regards

Ivan

2

Sample answer:

Hi Siobhan

I'm afraid that I need to take some time off work today for personal reasons.

If I can have today off, I will work on Saturday to catch up.

Please call me at home if you have any questions.

Kind regards

Alison

Unit 16 Personal profiles on networking sites

Looking closely

1

1 Alex is writing for a work social networking site (this site is used for looking for jobs, recommending colleagues and posting CVs).

2 Sarah is writing for a friend-finding social networking site (this site is used for looking for new friends).
3 Alex: confident, hardworking, great communication skills
Sarah: fun-loving, kind, confident, generous

Language focus

1

Note: these are suggested answers.

More suitable for work	More suitable for friends	Suitable for both
hardworking, experienced, qualified	musical, fun-loving, shy, generous, kind	confident, ambitious

2

1 experienced
2 musical
3 qualified
4 hardworking
5 confident
6 fun-loving
7 kind
8 shy
9 generous
10 ambitious

3

Students' own answers.

4

1 I have excellent writing skills.
2 I'm ambitious and confident.
3 I have three years' experience as a waiter.
4 I'm a qualified project manager.

5

Sample answers:

I'm a qualified lawyer with three years' experience. I'm hardworking and ambitious and I have excellent communication skills. I've worked in two different countries.

Looking closely

1

1 OK
2 TP
3 TH
4 OK
5 TH
6 TP

Get writing

1

Sample answer:

I'm a confident, ambitious and hardworking manager. I have four years' experience in the catering industry. I have managed restaurants in Amsterdam and London. I have excellent communication skills and can speak four languages.

2

Sample answer:

I'm a fun-loving, kind and generous person. I'm musical – I love playing guitar and going to concerts. I love my friends and family and spend a lot of time travelling. I'm looking for new friends to go for coffee and concerts with.

Unit 17   Blogging

Looking closely

1

1 Eva's blog is about her life in London.
2 Eva is studying fashion (clothes design) at a college.
3 In a blog, the most recent post always comes first. The oldest post appears at the bottom of the page.

Language focus

1

Phrases and sentences for describing places:

London is great! It's expensive to live here but there is so much to see and do. My flat is in Shoreditch – probably the coolest place in East London. There are lots of fun cafés and bars.

Phrases and sentences for describing people:
Everyone is so friendly. People wear really strange and interesting clothes here.

2

Nouns	Adjectives that can describe the nouns
1 buildings	glass, modern, cool, interesting, wooden, old, exciting
2 places	busy, modern, cool, interesting, noisy, exciting, fun, old, friendly, beautiful
3 houses	glass, modern, cool, interesting, wooden, fun, old, beautiful
4 people	busy, modern, cool, interesting, noisy, exciting, fun, old, friendly, beautiful
5 things to do	cool, interesting, exciting, fun

3

1 buildings
2 modern
3 house
4 noisy
5 interesting
6 cool

4

Students' own answers.

Language focus

1

1	are	3	took	5	didn't
2	enjoys	4	drove	6	saw

2

Sentences in the past simple: Last night I went to see a music concert. I had a great time. I moved into my flat, started my course and met lots of new people. I was a bit scared of the traffic at first…

3

Sample answers:

1 I'm in Vermont. The countryside here is very beautiful.
2 Last weekend I went to Margate – a town in Kent near the sea. I visited an amazing art gallery.
3 I live in a tower block. It's a very modern building.

Get writing

1

Sample answer:

The City

Most of the buildings here are quite modern. But some houses are made from wood and are over 100 years old.

Everyone here is busy. People are very noisy. They aren't very friendly! It takes a long time to make friends here – my best friends are from my home country.

People here love to sit outside cafés in the summer, and to take long walks beside the river. I go to a lot of concerts and art galleries.

2

Sample answer:

My trip to Dalian, China

Dalian is a lovely city in the north of China. It is next to the sea, so there is lots of beautiful countryside close to the city. There are lots of modern buildings, including glass 'skyscrapers' (very tall buildings). There are some older buildings on quiet streets with lots of trees.

On Sunday I went for a long walk by the sea. It was very warm, and lots of people were sunbathing and swimming. A man and woman were getting married and they had their wedding photos taken on the beach!

Last night I went out to a seafood restaurant and ate some delicious seafood. The people are very friendly and I met some Chinese and Russian people.

Unit 18   Twitter

Looking closely

1

1 New York City. We know because he mentions it in his first Tweet and shares a link to a photo of it.
2 They are probably friends (they go cycling together) but not best friends (Anton didn't know Dayo was on holiday).
3 She is sharing information about a traffic jam (lots of cars and other vehicles making it hard to drive anywhere fast). She is probably sharing the information to help other drivers to stay away from the traffic jam.
4 She is a teacher. We know because her Twitter name is @TeacherinRome and because she talks about her students in her Tweet.

2

1 a person's Twitter name
2 a Tweet
3 a reply
4 a repeat (Retweet) of something someone else has Tweeted
5 a hashtag (#)
6 a link
7 how long since the Tweet was posted

Language focus

1

1	sport	3	celebrities	5	politics
2	weather	4	events		

2

Sample answers:

1 President of the Philippines flies to China to talk about the future of both countries.
2 Brazil beats Italy by three goals to two.
3 Madonna flies to London to begin her European concerts/tour.

Language focus

1

1	RT	3	@	5	weather
2	#	4	Janice		

2

Sample answers:

1   #weather #snow
2   #politics #Denmark #Germany
3   #sport #Olympics #Phelps #swimming
4   #cat #funny #amazing
5   #tickets #Rihanna

Get writing

1

Sample answers:

1   RT @sportsfan23456 That was the best hockey match I've ever seen!
2   @KathrynAnneW Sorry! I don't have one either.
3   @IloveLondon36 It's cold and wet in Inverness today! I'm staying inside ☹
4   @KathrynAnneW I Just saw a tweet from @radioheadfan476. You can get new Radiohead tickets from: shortlink.com/Radiohead/tickets

2

Students' own answers.

Unit 19   Social media

Looking closely

1

1   She is probably happy because she has just been on a trip to Paris.
2   Anja and Christopher are colleagues at work.
3   Darren is sad. We know because he uses the word 'terrible' and a sad face emoticon.
4   'Check out' means 'look at' this gallery website.

2

1   profile picture
2   tag
3   'Like button'
4   comment
5   post
6   link

Language focus

1

1   posted
2   links
3   profile
4   tag
5   timeline/wall

2

| 1 | C | 3 | R | 5 | S/R |
| 2 | C | 4 | S | 6 | S |

3

Comments in the correct order: 2,5,3,1,4

4

Photo 1: (b) Mr Tibbles looking very cute and fluffy.

Photo 2: (c) Everyone having a great time at Miranda's party.

Photo 3: (d) Grandpa's 85th birthday!

Photo 4: (a) Cameron running the half marathon yesterday. So proud of him!

Get writing

1

Sample answers:

Photo 1: 1 Julian kayaking in Canada

Photo 2: 2 Millie at her graduation.

2

Sample answers:

1   I'd love the ticket, Matthew!
2   Oh no! I think there's another library in Dundee. Maybe you could go there instead?
3   Happy Birthday Darren! See you tonight!

Unit 20   Online reviews

Looking closely

1

1   Benny's Diner is probably a fast food restaurant.
2   A rating is a score or a number you give to something when you review it. 4/5 (pronounced 'four out of five') is a good rating. 0/5 is a very bad rating.
3   He means that the people who work at the hostel do not do a good job.

1

	Good points	**Bad points**
Benny's Diner	food really good, kids enjoyed burgers and milkshakes, waiter was really friendly, menu is good and not too expensive	fries were quite cold, service was quite slow (waited half an hour for food)
Downton Youth Hostel	quite quiet	terrible service, no one to clean the rooms, manager is really rude, expensive

Language focus

1

Adverb + adjective combinations: really good, quite cold, really friendly, quite slow, absolutely terrible, really rude, quite quiet

2

1   The food in the restaurant was absolutely terrible.
2   The food at the restaurant was quite nice.
3   The Youth Hostel was really great.
4   The service at my local café is very good.
5   That hotel is quite clean.
6   I really like that Thai restaurant.

3

Students' own answers.

4

1 f   3 e   5 a   7 h
2 b   4 d   6 c   8 g

5

1   youth hostel   4   service   7   staff
2   manager   5   rating   8   waiter
3   menu   6   price

6

1   clean   4   rude   7   waiter
2   friendly   5   large   expensive
3   cheap   6   cheap

7

Sample answers:

1   We really wouldn't recommend that Brazilian restaurant. The food is terrible!
2   I really liked the New Street Hotel. The rooms were very clean.
3   Tapas Ole! is a bad restaurant. The food is really terrible and the prices are expensive.
4   I would recommend the Charter Street Youth Hostel. The rooms are large and the staff are quite friendly.

Get writing

1

Sample answer:

My local café is great. The menu is small but the prices are cheap and the food is really good. The manager and the waiters and waitresses are all really friendly. The only thing I don't like is that service can be quite slow – especially on a Saturday when the café is really busy.

Rating 4/5

2

Sample answer:

The Excelsior Hotel is quite good. The staff are friendly and the service is OK. The rooms are large and clean and the prices are really cheap.

The best thing about the Excelsior is the restaurant. The food is absolutely amazing. You must try it!

Rating 4/5.